THE
CATALYST

How to Change Anyone's Mind

Jonah Berger

Simon & Schuster

New York   London   Toronto   Sydney   New Delhi

Simon & Schuster
1230 Avenue of the Americas
New York, NY 10020

First Simon & Schuster hardcover edition March 2020

SIMON & SCHUSTER and colophon are registered trademarks
of Simon & Schuster, Inc.

For information about special discounts for bulk purchases,
please contact Simon & Schuster Special Sales at 1-866-506-1949
or business@simonandschuster.com.

The Simon & Schuster Speakers Bureau can bring authors to
your live event. For more information or to book an event,
contact the Simon & Schuster Speakers Bureau at 1-866-248-3049
or visit our website at www.simonspeakers.com.

Printed in Canada

10 9 8 7 6 5 4

Library of Congress Cataloging-in-Publication Data
Names: Berger, Jonah, author.
Title: The catalyst : how to change anyone's mind / Jonah Berger.
Description: New York : Simon & Schuster, [2020] | Includes
    bibliographical references and index. | Summary: "From the author
    of *New York Times* bestsellers *Contagious* and *Invisible Influence*
    comes a revolutionary approach to changing anyone's mind"—
    Provided by publisher.
Identifiers: LCCN 2019044601 | ISBN 9781982108601 (hardcover) |
    ISBN 9781982108649 (paperback) | ISBN 9781982108656 (ebook)
Subjects: LCSH: Change (Psychology) | Persuasion (Psychology)
Classification: LCC BF637.C4 B458 2020 | DDC 303.3/42—dc23
LC record available at https://lccn.loc.gov/2019044601

ISBN 978-1-9821-0860-1
ISBN 978-1-9821-0865-6 (ebook)

To Jordan, Jasper, Zoë, and little piccolina
For changing my life in all the best ways

Contents

THE
CATALYST

Introduction

As a case agent for the FBI, Greg Vecchi specialized in international drug trafficking, money laundering, and extortion. Many of his targets were hardened, violent career criminals. The kinds of guys who sold helicopters to the Medellín drug cartel or tried to buy old Russian submarines to sneak cocaine into the United States from Colombia.

To corner one suspect from the Russian mob, Greg led a three-year wiretapping effort, painstakingly collecting information and building a case. When the warrants were ready, Greg called in a SWAT team: dozens of stocky guys in full body armor who would then storm in, neutralize the bad guys, and collect the evidence.

As he briefed the team, he outlined the various concerns. Greg emphasized that the suspect might be armed and was certainly dangerous. The SWAT team formed an arrest plan that left no room for error. They needed to get this just right or things could turn violent in a hurry.

At the end of the briefing, everyone left the room except for one guy. Greg had spotted him earlier. In a room full of commandos, this guy looked out of place. Fat, short, and bald, he was nowhere close to the chiseled picture of SWAT material.

"Tell me about your guy," the man asked. "I want to know more."

"Not sure what you mean," said Greg. "I just did. I said I've got this whole file of—"

"No. No, no, no," went the guy. "I don't mean his criminal history. I don't mean his violent past and all the other stuff. You've been on the wiretap, right?"

"Yeah," Greg replied.

"What is he like?" the man asked.

"What do you mean, 'What is he like'?"

"What does he do? What are his hobbies? Tell me about his family. Does he have any pets?"

Does the suspect have any pets? Greg thought to himself. *We're about to send a paramilitary unit after a guy, and you want to know whether he has any pets? What a bunch of crap. No wonder this guy got left behind by the rest of the SWAT team.*

Greg dutifully provided the information and started to collect the briefing documents he'd laid out.

"One last question," the guy said. "The suspect is there now, right?"

"Yeah," said Greg.

"Well, give me his phone number," the guy said, before walking out the door.

When it came time for the arrest, the SWAT team was ready. Stacked in a line outside the building, one behind the other, waiting to kick in the door. Dressed in black from head to toe, they had their shields out and guns drawn. "Get down! Get down! Get down!" they'd yell before rushing in and grabbing the suspect.

But as the seconds ticked by, the SWAT team still hadn't gone in. A few minutes passed. Then a few more.

Greg started to worry. He knew the suspect better than anyone. He'd listened to him talk with his friends and associates. The guy was bad news. He would kill people. He'd been in a Russian prison and he wasn't scared of a fight.

Then all of a sudden the door opened up.

And out into the open came the suspect. With his hands up.

Greg was dumbfounded. He'd been in law enforcement for a long time. Years as a special agent in the U.S. Army and the Department of Agriculture. He'd worked undercover across the United States and done anti-corruption work on the Mexican border. He had a good chunk of experience. But a guy coming out of his own accord and getting arrested without incident? He'd never seen anything like it.

Then he realized: that short, bald guy he'd been talking to? *That* guy was a hostage negotiator. And the hostage negotiator convinced the suspect to do something no one thought possible: turn himself over to the authorities, in broad daylight, without a fight.

Shit, Greg thought. *I want to be that guy.*

Since then Greg has spent more than twenty years as a hostage negotiator. He's dealt with international kidnappings, interviewed Saddam Hussein after his capture, and headed the FBI's legendary Behavioral Science Unit. From talking down bank robbers to interrogating serial killers, he's changed people's minds under seemingly impossible conditions.

Crisis negotiation emerged after the 1972 Munich Olympic

Games, where terrorists took hostage and then killed eleven Israeli Olympians. Previously, the focus had often been on force, telling people, "Come out with your hands up or we'll shoot!" But after Munich and a number of other very public failures, it became clear that bullying people into submission wasn't working. So practitioners turned to the psychology literature, using behavioral science to build new training techniques that could safely deescalate a crisis.[1]

For the last few decades, negotiators like Greg have relied on a different model—one that works. Whether trying to convince an international terrorist to let hostages go or to change someone's mind about committing suicide. Even when talking to someone who just killed his family, who's locked himself up in a bank with hostages, who knows he's talking to a police officer, who knows the consequences and knows his life is going to change. Nine out of ten times he comes out by himself.

And he comes out just because someone asks.

The Power of Inertia

Everyone has something they want to change. Salespeople want to change their customers' minds and marketers want to change purchase decisions. Employees want to change their bosses' perspective and leaders want to change organizations. Parents want to change their children's behavior. Start-ups want to change industries. Nonprofits want to change the world.

But change is hard.

We persuade and cajole and pressure and push, but even after all that work, often nothing moves. Things change at a glacial pace if they change at all. In the tale of the tortoise and the hare, change is a three-toed sloth on his lunch break.

Isaac Newton famously noted that an object in motion tends to stay in motion, while an object at rest tends to stay at rest. Sir Isaac focused on physical objects—planets, pendulums, and the like—but the same concepts can be applied to the social world. Just like moons and comets, people and organizations are guided by conservation of momentum. Inertia. They tend to do what they've always done.

Rather than thinking about which candidate represents their values, voters tend to pick whoever represents the party they voted for in the past. Rather than starting fresh and thinking about which projects deserve attention, companies take last year's budget and use that as a starting point. Rather than rebalancing financial portfolios, investors tend to look at how they've been investing and stay the course.

Inertia explains why families go back to the same vacation spot every year and why organizations are wary of starting new initiatives but loath to kill off old ones.

When trying to change minds and overcome such inertia, the tendency is to push. Client not buying the pitch? Send them a deck of facts and reasons. Boss not listening to the idea? Give them more examples or a deeper explanation.

Whether trying to change company culture or get the kids to eat their vegetables, the assumption is that pushing harder will do the trick. That if we just provide more information, more facts, more reasons, more arguments, or just add a little more force, people will change.

Implicitly, this approach assumes that people are like marbles. Push them in one direction and they will go that way.

Unfortunately, that approach often backfires. Unlike marbles, people don't just roll with it when you try to push them. They push back. Rather than saying yes, the client stops returning our calls. Rather than going along, the boss says they'll think about it, which is a nice way of saying "Thanks, but no way." Rather than coming out with their hands up, a suspect holes up and starts shooting.

So if pushing people doesn't work, what does?

A Better Way to Change Minds

To answer this question, it helps to look to a completely different domain: chemistry.

Left to itself, chemical change can take eons. Algae and plankton turning into oil, or carbon being gradually squeezed into diamonds. For reactions to occur, molecules must break the bonds between their atoms and form new ones. It's a slow and painstaking process that happens over thousands if not millions of years.

To facilitate change, chemists often use a special set of substances. These unsung heroes clean the exhaust in your car and the grime on your contact lenses. They turn air into fertilizer and petroleum into bike helmets. They speed change, enabling molecules that might take years to interact to do so in seconds.

Most intriguing, though, is the *way* these substances generate change.

Chemical reactions usually require a certain amount of energy. Turning nitrogen gas into fertilizer, for example, usually requires heating things up to over 1000°C. Adding enough energy, through temperature and pressure, to force a reaction.

Special substances speed up the process. But rather than upping the heat or adding more pressure, they provide an alternate route, reducing the amount of energy required for reactions to occur.

At first glance, this seems impossible. Like magic. How can

faster change happen with *less* energy? It seems to violate the very laws of thermodynamics.

But special substances take a different approach. Rather than pushing, they lower the barriers to change.

And these substances are called catalysts.*

Catalysts have revolutionized chemistry. Their discovery generated multiple Nobel Prizes, kept billions of people from starving, and spawned some of the greatest inventions of the last few centuries.

But their underlying approach is equally powerful in the social world. Because there is a better way to generate change. It's not about pushing harder. And it's not about being more convincing or a better persuader. These tactics might work once in a while, but more often than not they just lead people to up their defenses.

Instead, it's about being a catalyst—changing minds by removing roadblocks and lowering the barriers that keep people from taking action.

That's exactly what hostage negotiators do. Anyone faced with a SWAT team bearing down on them is bound to feel trapped. Whether they're a Russian mobster or a would-be bank robber holding three hostages at gunpoint. Push them too hard and they'll snap. Tell them what to do and they're unlikely to listen.

---

* Reactions happen when molecules collide. But rather than increasing the frequency of collisions, as adding energy does, catalysts increase their success rate. Instead of bouncing around on a bunch of blind dates, hoping something sticks, a catalyst acts as a matchmaker, encouraging reactants to encounter each other at the right orientations for change to occur.

Good hostage negotiators take a different tack. They start by listening and building trust. They encourage the suspect to talk through their fears and motivations and who's waiting for them back home. Even talking about *pets* in the middle of a tense stand-off, if that is what's required.

Because the hostage negotiators' aim is to ease the pressure, rather than banging down the door. Gradually lowering the suspect's fear, uncertainty, and hostility, until they look at their situation and realize that the best option is likely the one that seemed unthinkable at the start: coming out with their hands up.

Great hostage negotiators don't push harder. Or up the heat in an already tense situation. Instead, they identify what's preventing change from happening and remove that barrier. Allowing change to happen with less energy, not more.

Just like a catalyst.

Catalyzing Change

I started studying catalysts because I was stuck.

A Fortune 500 company had asked for help launching a revolutionary new product, but traditional approaches weren't working. They'd tried advertising, push messaging, and all the usual tactics, without much luck.

So I dug into the literature.

In my day job, as a professor at the Wharton School at the University of Pennsylvania, I've spent more than two decades studying the science of social influence, word of mouth, and why things become popular. With a set of amazing colleagues, I've conducted hundreds of experiments on everything from why people buy to what drives decision-making and choice. I've had the pleasure of teaching tens of thousands of students and executives, and helped hundreds of companies like Apple, Google, Nike, and GE change minds, behaviors, and actions. I've helped Facebook launch new hardware, the Bill & Melinda Gates Foundation sharpen messaging, and small start-ups, political campaigns, and nonprofit organizations get their products, services, and ideas to catch on.

But as I read more and more, I realized that most perspectives out there took the same traditional approach. Coax, convince, and encourage. Push, push, push. And if that doesn't work, rinse and repeat. Step on the gas and push harder.

And they weren't working.

I started wondering if there might be a better way. I interviewed start-up founders to learn how they drive adoption of new products and services. I talked with CEOs and managers to discover how great leaders transform organizations. I spoke to superstar salespeople to learn how they convince the toughest clients. And I consulted with public health officials to find out how they change behavior and speed diffusion of important medical innovations.

Slowly, a different method emerged. An alternate approach to changing minds.

We tried a rough version with the client and it got a little traction. We revised it and were even more successful. Emboldened by these early wins, we tried extending the approach to a different company. They found it useful, and soon I was trying this technique on all my consulting projects. Driving product adoption, changing behavior, and shifting organizational culture.

One day a potential client asked if I had something written up that I could share. Something that documented our strategy and approach.

I culled slides from different PowerPoint decks but realized that wasn't enough. There needed to be one place where all the information was pulled together in an easy-to-read package.

This is that place.

Find the Parking Brakes

This book takes a different approach to change.

Unfortunately, when it comes to trying to create change, people rarely think about removing roadblocks. When asked how to change someone's mind, 99 percent of the answers focus on some version of pushing. "Present facts and evidence," "Explain my reasons," and "Convince them" are common refrains.

We are so focused on our desired outcome that we're consumed with how we can push people in that direction. But along the way, we tend to forget about the person whose mind we're trying to change. And what's stopping them.

Because rather than asking what might convince someone to change, catalysts start with a more basic question: *Why hasn't that person changed already?* What is blocking them?

That's what this book is all about: how to overcome inertia, incite action, and change minds—not by being more persuasive, or pushing harder, but by being a catalyst. By removing the barriers to change.

Every time you start driving, you buckle your seat belt, stick your key in the ignition, and slowly press the gas pedal. Sometimes, if you're on an incline, the car needs a little more gas, but in general the more you push on the gas, the more movement you get.

But what if you push and push and the car doesn't budge? Then what?

Whenever change fails to happen, we think we need more

horsepower. Employees not adopting that new strategy? Send out another email reminding them why they should. Customers not buying the product? Spend more money on advertising or give them yet another sales call.

But with all that focus on pushing on the gas, we often overlook an easier and more effective way: identifying what is blocking or preventing change. And eliminating these obstacles to action.

Sometimes change doesn't require more horsepower. Sometimes we just need to unlock the parking brake.

This book is about finding the parking brakes. Discovering the hidden barriers preventing change. Identifying the root or core issues that are thwarting action and learning how to mitigate them.

Each chapter lays out a key roadblock and how to address it.

Principle 1: Reactance

When pushed, people push back. Just like a missile defense system protects against incoming projectiles, people have an innate anti-persuasion system. Radar that kicks in when they sense someone is trying to convince them. To lower this barrier, catalysts encourage people to persuade themselves. You'll learn about the science of reactance, how warnings become recommendations, and the power of tactical empathy. How a public health official got teens to quit smoking and how a hostage negotiator got hardened criminals to come out with their hands up, just by asking.

Principle 2: Endowment

As the old saying goes, if it ain't broke, don't fix it. People are wedded to what they're already doing. And unless what they're doing is terrible, they don't want to switch. To ease endowment, or people's attachment to the status quo, catalysts highlight how inaction isn't as costless as it seems. Discover why sellers value things more than buyers, why the upsides need to be 2.6 times larger than the downsides to get people to take action, and why spraining a finger can actually be more painful than breaking one. How financial advisors get clients to invest more sensibly and how IT professionals get employees to adopt new technologies.

Principle 3: Distance

People have an innate anti-persuasion system, but even when we just provide information, sometimes it backfires. Why? Another barrier is distance. If new information is within people's zone of acceptance, they're willing to listen. But if it is too far away, in the region of rejection, everything flips. Communication is ignored or, even worse, increases opposition. You'll learn how to swing a voter and how a political activist got committed conservatives to support liberal policies like transgender rights. Why big changes require asking for less, not pushing for more. And how catalysts find the unsticking points to change minds on the seemingly toughest issues.

Principle 4: Uncertainty

Change often involves uncertainty. Will a new product, service, or idea be as good as the old one? It's hard to know for sure, and this uncertainty makes people hit the pause button, halting action. To overcome this barrier, catalysts make things easier to try. Like free samples at the supermarket or test drives at the car dealership, reducing risk by letting people experience things for themselves. Discover why lenient return policies increase profits, why farmers fail to adopt helpful innovations, and how a former minor-league baseball ticket salesman built a billion-dollar business on free shipping. And lest you think this idea is restricted to big businesses with a product or service to offer, I'll show you how anyone can apply these concepts, from animal shelters and accountants to vegetarians and organizational change efforts.

Principle 5: Corroborating Evidence

Sometimes one person, no matter how knowledgeable or assured, is not enough. Some things just need more proof. More evidence to overcome the translation problem and drive change. Sure, one person endorsed something, but what does their endorsement say about whether *I'll* like it? To overcome this barrier, catalysts find reinforcement. Corroborating evidence. You'll see how substance abuse counselors encourage addicts to seek treatment, which sources are most impactful, and why and when it's better to concentrate scarce resources rather than spreading them out.

Reactance, Endowment, Distance, Uncertainty, and *Corroborating Evidence* can be called the five horsemen of inertia. Five key roadblocks that hinder or inhibit change.

Each chapter focuses on one of these roadblocks, and how to reduce it. Integrating research and case studies to illustrate the underlying science behind each roadblock and the principles that individuals and organizations have used to mitigate it.

These five ways to be a catalyst can be organized into an acronym. Catalysts reduce **R**eactance, ease **E**ndowment, shrink **D**istance, alleviate **U**ncertainty, and find **C**orroborating **E**vidence. Taken together, that forms an acronym, REDUCE. Which is exactly what great catalysts do. They **REDUCE** roadblocks. They change minds and incite action by reducing barriers to change.

After each principle, there is a short case study illustrating how these ideas apply to different domains—from changing the boss's mind and driving Britons to support Brexit to changing consumer behavior and getting a grand dragon to renounce the Ku Klux Klan.

Note that not every situation involves all five roadblocks. Sometimes reactance is the key barrier. Other times uncertainty plays a larger role. Some cases involve a combination of a few barriers, and others involve only one. But by understanding all of them, we can diagnose which ones are at work and mitigate them.

This book has a simple goal: to reframe how we approach a universal problem. You'll learn why people and organizations change—and how you can catalyze that process.

Throughout the book I'll apply the idea of removing barriers to individual, organizational, and social change. And along the way you'll see how catalysts have applied these ideas to a range of different situations. How leaders transform organizational culture and how activists ignite social movements. How salespeople close the deal and employees get management to support new ideas. How substance abuse counselors get addicts to realize they have a problem and how political canvassers change deeply rooted political beliefs.

We'll talk about changing both minds and behavior. Sometimes concepts that change one also change the other, but other times we don't need to change minds to drive action. Sometimes people are already open to changing their behavior; we just need to remove roadblocks and make it easier to happen.

This book is designed for anyone who wants to catalyze change. It provides a powerful way of thinking and a range of techniques that can lead to extraordinary results.

Whether you're trying to change one person, transform an organization, or shift the way an entire industry does business, this book will teach you how to become a catalyst.[2]

1. Reactance

Chuck Wolfe was facing an impossible task. Florida's governor had asked him to head up a new program. This itself was nothing new. Chuck had served the governor for almost a decade in a variety of different roles: operations manager, director of external affairs, and executive director of financial oversight. He had developed and implemented programs that aided relief efforts after Hurricane Andrew and helped the city of Miami dig itself out of its financial crisis.

But this time the challenge was much larger. Chuck's job was to build a team to fight an industry that sold more than a trillion products to more than a billion consumers worldwide. An industry that spent almost $10 billion a year marketing its products and in which leading companies individually had profits larger than Coca-Cola, Microsoft, and McDonald's.

Combined.

Chuck's goal? To do something dozens of organizations had failed at for decades: to get teens to stop smoking.

In the late 1990s, smoking was the biggest public health crisis facing the nation. Cigarettes were the largest cause of preventable deaths and disease, killing tens of millions of people worldwide. In the United States alone, smoking was responsible for one in five deaths and had an economic cost of almost $150 billion a year.[1]

The problem was particularly acute among teens. Tobacco companies knew the youth market was vital to their success. While outwardly they claimed to avoid teens and children, internally they knew that wasn't an option. "Today's teenager is tomorrow's potential regular customer, and the overwhelming majority of smokers first begin to smoke while still in their teens," a Philip Morris memo noted. Not selling to children meant going out of business.

So companies used all manner of devices to appeal to the younger demographic. When the *Flintstones* cartoon debuted in 1960, Winston cigarettes was the sponsor, and commercials showed Fred and Barney Rubble taking cigarette breaks. When advertising on television and radio was banned in the early 1970s, cigarette companies invented friendly cartoon characters like Joe Camel to make cigarettes seem fun. And when regular cigarettes didn't seem attractive enough for younger palates, they introduced flavored tobacco in colorful candy wrappers to make the product more appealing.

It worked.

Teen smoking rates should be low. Federal law requires that people be at least eighteen to purchase cigarettes in the United States, and most students don't reach that age until midway through their last year of high school. Some cities have raised the age even higher.

But by the late 1990s, things looked ominous. Almost three-quarters of high school students had smoked.[2] One in four seniors reported smoking daily. Teen smoking was at a nineteen-year high. And the numbers were increasing.

Someone needed to shut teen smoking down. And fast.

But stopping teens smoking was no easy task. Organizations had tried—and failed—for decades. Countries banned cigarette advertising. They added health warnings to tobacco packaging. And they spent billions of dollars trying to persuade young people to quit.

But despite all these efforts, smoking rates actually increased.[3]

How could Chuck Wolfe succeed when everything else had failed?

When Warnings Become Recommendations

To answer that question, it helps to understand why prior warnings fell short. And what better way to do that than examine a warning that shouldn't have even been necessary in the first place?

In early 2018, Procter & Gamble had a small PR problem.

Fifty years earlier they had launched Salvo, a granular laundry detergent compacted into tablet form. The tablets weren't that successful, but after decades of work, Procter & Gamble had a new formulation that they thought would be more effective. Rather than having to measure out exactly how much detergent to use, or risk getting a sticky mess on their clothes, consumers could just pull one of these small self-encased bubbles from a box and toss it into the washing machine. The plastic would dissolve in the water, releasing the detergent only when needed. No muss, no fuss.

Procter & Gamble introduced the product under the Tide brand, called them Tide Pods, and launched them with the promise of making laundry easier. The company invested more than $150 million in marketing, believing that the pods could ultimately capture 30 percent of the $6.5 billion U.S. laundry detergent market.

There was only one problem: people were eating them.

The Tide Pod Challenge, as it was called, started as a joke. Someone remarked that the bright orange and blue swirls looked good enough to eat, and after an *Onion* article ("So Help Me God, I'm Going to Eat One of Those Multicolored Detergent Pods"), a CollegeHumor video, and various social media posts, a buzz started.

Now people were challenging others to eat detergent. Teens would shoot videos of themselves chewing or gagging on the pods and post them on YouTube, daring others to do the same. In feats of culinary inspiration, some were even cooking the pods before ingesting them.[4]

Soon everyone from Fox News to the *Washington Post* was covering the craze. Doctors were brought in to comment, parents wrung their hands, and everyone puzzled over the odd trend that was picking up steam.

So Procter & Gamble did what many companies would do in this situation. They told people not to do it.

On January 12, 2018, Tide tweeted "What should Tide PODs be used for? DOING LAUNDRY. Nothing else.

Eating a Tide POD is a BAD IDEA . . ."

To make things even clearer, Tide enlisted celebrity football player Rob "Gronk" Gronkowski to help. In a short video, Tide asks Gronk whether eating Tide Pods is *ever* a good idea. His answer is simple. "NO, NO, NO, NO, NO, NO," Gronk says as he shakes his finger at the camera and the screen fills with "NOs." "Not even as a joke?" they ask. "NO, NO, NO, NO, NO," Gronk replies. "Should you use Tide Pods for anything but cleaning clothes?" they say. "NO," says Gronk.

The video closes with a warning: "Laundry packs are highly concentrated detergent meant only to clean clothes." And as if that weren't unambiguous enough, they add a quote from Gronk: "Do not eat."

For good measure, a couple hours later Gronk himself followed up on social media. "I've partnered with @Tide to make sure you know, Tide PODs are for doing laundry," he tweeted. "Nothing else!"

And that's when all hell broke loose.

Warning people about health risks has been a standard approach for decades. Eat less fat. Don't drink and drive. Wear your seat belt. Pick any health concern, add an admonishment to do it (if it's good) or not do it (if it's bad), and you've basically captured the essence of public health messaging for the last fifty years.

So it's no surprise that Procter & Gamble thought this is what they should do. The Tide execs probably thought it was ridiculous that they had to say anything in the first place. Who would think that eating something filled with alcohol ethoxy sulfate and propylene glycol would be a good idea? After all, the website already had a helpful note saying, "Keep out of reach of children." Enlisting Gronk to tell people not to eat the pods should help spread the word and stem any doubt.

But that's not what happened.

Right after Gronk and Tide warned people not to eat them, Google searches for Tide Pods spiked to their highest level ever.

Four days later they had more than doubled. Within a week they were up almost 700 percent.

Unfortunately, the traffic wasn't from concerned parents trying to figure out why Tide had taken to Twitter to remind people of the obvious. Visits to poison control centers shot up as well.

In all of 2016, there had been only thirty-nine cases of teens ingesting, inhaling, or absorbing laundry packets. In a dozen days following the Tide announcement, there were twice that many. Within a few months the number had more than doubled that of the prior two years combined.

Tide's efforts had backfired.

The Tide Pod Challenge might seem unusual, but it's actually an example of a much broader phenomenon.[5] Instructing jurors to disregard inadmissible testimony can encourage them to weigh it more heavily. Alcohol prevention messages can lead college students to drink more. And trying to persuade people that smoking is bad for their health can actually make them more interested in smoking in the future.

In these and similar examples, warnings became recommendations. Just as telling a teenager not to date someone somehow makes that person more alluring, telling people *not* to do something has the opposite effect: it makes them *more* likely to do it.

The Need for Freedom and Autonomy

In the late 1970s, researchers from Harvard and Yale published a study that helps explain why warnings backfire.

Working with a local nursing home called the Arden House, they conducted a simple experiment.[6] On one floor, residents were reminded of how much freedom and control they had over their lives. They could choose how they wanted their rooms to be arranged and whether they wanted the staff to help them rearrange the furniture. They could decide how they wanted to spend their time and whether they wanted to visit other residents or do something else. And they were reminded that if they had any complaints, they could provide feedback so that things would change.

To underscore their autonomy, these residents were given some additional choices. A box of houseplants was passed around, and residents were asked whether they wanted a plant to take care of, and, if so, which one. A movie was being shown two nights the following week, and residents were asked which night they wanted to go, if they wanted to go at all.

On another floor, residents received a similar speech but without the inclusion of freedom and control. They were reminded that the staff had set up their rooms to try to make them as happy as possible. They were handed houseplants and told the nurses would take care of them on their behalf. And they were reminded there was a movie the following week and told they would be assigned to watch it one day or the other.

After some time passed, researchers followed up to see how residents were doing and whether the reminders had any effect.

The results were striking. Residents who had been given more control were more cheerful, active, and alert.

But even more astonishing were the longer-term effects. Eighteen months later the researchers examined mortality rates across the two groups. On the floor that had been given more freedom and control, less than half as many residents had died. Feeling that they had more autonomy seemed to make people live longer.

ple have a need for freedom and autonomy. To feel that their lives and actions are within their personal control. That, rather than driven by randomness, or subject to the whims of others, they get to choose.

Consequently, people are loath to give up agency. In fact, choice is so important that people prefer it even when it makes them worse off. Even when having choice makes them less happy.

In one study,[7] researchers asked people to imagine being the parents of Julie, a premature baby admitted to a hospital's neo-natal intensive care unit with a brain hemorrhage. Julie's life was being sustained by a ventilator, but unfortunately, after three weeks of treatment, her health had not improved. Consequently, the doctors summoned Julie's parents to explain the situation.

There were two options: stop the treatment, which meant Julie would die, or continue the treatment, although Julie might die anyway. Even if she survived, she would suffer crippling neu-rological impairment. Both options were far from ideal.

Participants were divided into two groups. One group was asked to make the choice themselves. Whether to stop treatment or continue it.

The other group was told that the doctors made the decision for them. They were told that the doctors had decided it was in Julie's best interest to stop the treatment.

This is clearly a terrible situation to be in. Whether people made the choice themselves or the doctors made it for them, all participants felt nervous, upset, distressed—and guilty.

But researchers found that the choosers felt worse. Having to personally choose whether to pull the plug made the situation feel all the more awful.

That said, choosers still didn't want to give up control. When asked, they said they preferred making the decision themselves rather than letting the doctor decide. Even though it made them feel worse, they still wanted to have control.

Reactance and the Anti-Persuasion Radar

The choice study and the nursing home study help explain what happened with Procter & Gamble and the Tide Pods. People like to feel they have control over their choices and actions. That they have the freedom to drive their own behavior.

When others threaten or restrict that freedom, people get upset. When told they can't or shouldn't do something, it interferes with their autonomy. Their ability to see their actions as driven by themselves. So they push back: Who are you to tell me I can't text while driving or walk my dog on that pristine patch of grass? I can do whatever I want!

When people's ability to make their own choices is taken away or even threatened, they react against the potential loss of control. And one way to reassert that sense of control—to feel autonomous—is to engage in the forbidden behavior: to text while driving, let the dog loose on the grass, or even chomp down on some Tide Pods. Doing the forbidden thing becomes an easy way to reassert their sense of being in the driver's seat.[8]

While texting while driving might not have even been that attractive originally, threatening to restrict it makes it more desirable. The forbidden fruit tastes ever more sweet. And it tastes sweeter because eating it is a way to reclaim one's autonomy.

Restriction generates a psychological phenomenon called reactance. An unpleasant state that occurs when people feel their freedom is lost or threatened.

And reactance happens even when asking people to *do* something rather than telling them *not* to. Whether made to encourage people to buy a hybrid car or save money for retirement, any effort is often unintentionally seen as impinging on people's freedom. It interferes with their ability to see their behavior as driven by themselves.

In the absence of persuasion, people think they are doing what *they* want. They see their actions as driven by their own thoughts and preferences. The only reason they're interested in buying a hybrid car is because of these. They like helping the environment. They like the way the car looks.

Try to convince people, though, and things get more complex. Because now if they find themselves thinking of buying a hybrid, there is another explanation. In addition to their own inherent interest, now there is also a second possibility: maybe they're thinking about buying a hybrid because someone told them they should. And that alternate explanation for their interest threatens their perceived freedom. If they're considering buying a hybrid because someone told them they should, their behavior is not really being driven by themselves . They're not really in the driver's seat. Someone else is.

So, just like the Tide Pod Challenge, to reestablish a sense of autonomy, people often react against persuasion. They do the opposite of whatever is being requested.* Want me to buy a hy-

---

* People don't always react by doing the opposite of what is asked, but it's often the best way to feel that one hasn't been influenced. If an ad says, "Buy a hybrid from brand X," I could buy from brand Y instead, but I'd still be left with a nagging feeling that maybe the reason I bought a hybrid at all was the ad. But not buying one, or buying something completely different, like a pickup truck, avoids that attribution altogether: The ad asked

brid? No, thanks, I'll get a gas guzzler instead. Want me to sa money for retirement? I'll show you. I'll buy whatever I want![9] Pushing, telling, or just encouraging people to do something often makes them less likely to do it.

Reactance even happens when people had wanted to do what was suggested in the first place. Take a new workplace initiative to get people to speak up in meetings. Some people may want to speak up already, so the initiative should be an easy sell. People want to speak up; the company wants people to speak up; everybody wins.

But if the initiative crowds out people's ability to see their behavior as internally or freely driven, it can backfire. Someone who is thinking of speaking up now has an alternate explanation for that thought: that they're doing so not because they *want* to but because the initiative *told them* to. It interferes with their ability to see their decisions as their own. And if they don't want to feel like they're just going along with a directive, they might end up staying silent.

Just as a missile defense system protects a country against incoming projectiles, people have anti-persuasion radar. An innate anti-influence system that shields them from being swayed. They're constantly scanning the environment for influence attempts, and when they detect one, they deploy a set of countermeasures.[10] Responses that help them avoid being persuaded.

The simplest countermeasure is avoidance, or just ignoring

---

me to buy a hybrid, so not buying one must have been all me. The ad didn't say anything about a pickup truck, so if I buy one, I must be in the driver's seat. Doing anything other than what was requested provides some sense of freedom, but doing the opposite is often most effective.

the message. Leaving the room during a commercial, hanging up on a sales call, or shutting a pop-up window. Shoppers avoid salespeople and online shoppers avoid looking at banner ads. The more a commercial seems like it's trying to persuade people, the more likely they are to change the channel. By reducing exposure to incoming communication, its potential impact is weakened.

The more complex (and effortful) response is counterarguing. Rather than just ignoring the message, people actively contest it or work to combat it.

Take a message from Ford about its F-150 Truck: "CLASS-LEADING CAPABILITY . . . The Ford F-150 outperforms every other truck in its class when hauling cargo in the bed or towing a trailer. No wonder the competition is always in a scramble to follow the leader."

Rather than taking the message at face value, people contest its contents and source, scrutinizing the claims and arguing against them. Does the F-150 really have class-leading capability? Of course Ford would say that: they're trying to convince people to buy it. I bet Chevrolet says the same thing. Notice how they don't just say "outperforms every other truck." They qualify it with "in its class" and "when hauling cargo in the bed or towing a trailer." I wonder if it always outperforms the other trucks or only in a small set of specific situations. And what does "outperform" mean, anyway?

Like an overzealous high school debate team, people refute each claim and undermine the source. They poke and prod and raise objections until the message comes crumbling down.

Allow for Agency

To avoid reactance and the persuasion radar, then, catalysts allow for agency. They stop trying to persuade and instead get people to persuade themselves.

After Chuck Wolfe met with the governor, he put together a team to drive Florida's teen anti-smoking program.

The team knew that traditional advertising wouldn't work. Teens were savvy enough to know when someone was trying to convince them.

And they knew that health information by itself wouldn't solve the problem. It wasn't like teens thought smoking was healthy. Teens knew it was bad for them and they were doing it anyway.

So what was left?

After discussing various directions, Wolfe's team landed on a devastatingly simple idea. Something that had never been done before.

They stopped telling kids what to do.

For decades, adults had been telling kids not to smoke. Smoking is bad. Cigarettes will kill you. Stay away from them. Again and again and again.

Other public health campaigns had taken similar approaches.

Sure, there was some variation. Some appeals emphasized health ("Don't smoke: it will kill you") while others focused on vanity ("Don't smoke: it will give you yellow teeth"). Some highlighted athletics ("Don't smoke: it will make you worse at sports"), while others focused on peers ("Don't smoke: you'll get left out").

But, regardless of flavor or style, the subtext was the same. Whether explicit or not, there was always a request, demand, or suggested action: We know what's best for you and you should behave accordingly.

And it wasn't working.

So rather than assuming they had the answers, Wolfe's team asked teens for their perspective. In March 1998 they convened a Teen Tobacco Summit, where students came together to talk about and understand the problem.

And rather than tell teens smoking was bad, Chuck and the organizers let the teens take the lead. All the organizers did was lay out the facts: how the tobacco industry used manipulation and influence to sell cigarettes; how companies manipulated the political system and used sports, television, and movies to make smoking seem aspirational. Here is what the industry is doing, they said. You tell us what you want to do about it.

Many things came out of that summit. A new statewide organization called Students Working Against Tobacco, or SWAT, was formed to coordinate youth empowerment efforts. Workbooks were created to bring information about the tobacco industry into the classroom (e.g., if a carton of cigarettes generates $2 of profit, how much money would a tobacco executive make if they sold fourteen cartons of cigarettes?). And a different approach to media was formulated.

Take one of the first "truth" ads that ran soon after. Two regular teens, sitting in their regular-looking living room, call a magazine executive to ask why the publication accepted tobacco advertising, given they have a youth readership.

The executive says the magazine supports anti-tobacco ads, but when one of the teens asks whether the magazine would run some as a public service, the executive says no. When asked why not, he says, "We're in this business to make money." When the other teen asks, "Is this about people or about money?" the executive responds incredulously. "Publishing is about money," he says before quickly hanging up.

That's it.

The ad didn't demand anything from teens. There was no message at the end telling them not to smoke, what to do, or what would or wouldn't make them cool. The spot just let them know that, whether they realized it or not, cigarette companies were trying to influence them—and that the media was in on it. Rather than trying to persuade, the messages simply laid out the truth and left it up to teens to decide.

And decide they did.

In just a few months, the "truth campaign," as the program came to be known, led more than 30,000 Florida teens to quit smoking.[11] Within a couple years it cut teen smoking rates in half. It was the most effective large-scale prevention program. Ever.

The pilot program quickly became a worldwide model for youth tobacco control. When a national foundation was formed to eliminate teen smoking, it adopted Florida's strategy and converted "truth" into a national campaign. And it hired Chuck Wolfe to come on as its executive vice president.

Over the course of the national campaign, teen smoking rates dropped by 75 percent. Teens were less likely to start smoking, and those who already smoked were less likely to continue. The program prevented more than 450,000 youths from smoking in the first four years alone and saved tens of billions of dollars in health care costs.

In fact, the truth campaign was so effective in changing minds

2002 the program received one of strongest testaments to the success of their approach: Tobacco companies filed a lawsuit to stop it.

The truth campaign got teens to stop smoking because it didn't tell them to stop smoking. Wolfe understood that teens were smart enough to make their own decisions. But, more than that, he understood that by letting them make those decisions, rather than telling them what to do, they'd be more likely to make good decisions in the end.

Wolfe let teens chart their own path to his destination. By encouraging them to be active participants rather than passive bystanders, Chuck made them feel that they were in control. Lowering their radar and increasing action.[12]

To reduce reactance, catalysts allow for agency—not by telling people what to do or by being completely hands-off, but by finding the middle ground. By guiding their path.

Four key ways to do that are: (1) Provide a menu, (2) ask, don't tell, (3) highlight a gap, and (4) start with understanding.

Provide a Menu

One way to allow for agency is to let people pick the path. Let them choose how they get where you are hoping they'll go.

Parents use this idea all the time. Telling toddlers they have to eat a certain food usually fails. If they aren't interested in broccoli or chicken to begin with, pushing it on them is only going to build their resistance.

So, instead of pushing, savvy parents give their toddlers a choice: Which do you want to eat first, broccoli or chicken?

By giving kids options, the kids get to feel like they are in control: *Mom and Dad aren't telling me what to do; I'm picking what I want to eat.*

But by selecting the options Mom and Dad shape the decision. Little Liza is still eating the food she needs to be eating, just in the order she chooses.

You need to go to the doctor to get a shot; do you want it in the right or left arm? You need to get ready for bed; do you want to take a bath now or after you brush your teeth? *Guided choices* like these let children retain a sense of freedom and control while helping parents reach their desired outcomes.[13]

Smart bosses often do the same thing. Potential hires know they are supposed to negotiate, so—almost regardless of what they're offered—they usually ask for more.

One way to deal with this is to give candidates the tradeoffs. An extra week of vacation is equivalent to $5,000 less salary. Ten thousand more in salary is equivalent to this much less in equity.

Letting potential hires choose which dimension is more important makes them feel like they have more of an active role in the process[14]—and hopefully satisfies their need to negotiate. By letting candidates choose between two options the boss is equally happy with, potential hires feel like they have more autonomy without making the boss any worse off.

It's *providing a menu*: a limited set of options from which people can choose.

Go to most Italian restaurants for dinner, and there is more than one option available. Patrons can choose whether they want the spaghetti and meatballs or the lamb ragù. The Bolognese or the macadamia nut pesto.

Can consumers order anything they want? No. They can't

order sushi, egg rolls, lamb souvlaki, or any of several other things that the restaurant doesn't offer.

But within the limited set of things that are on the menu, they get to choose. It's choice, but it's bounded or guided choice. The restaurant sets the menu, and consumers choose within those bounds.

Advertising agencies do something similar when presenting work to clients. If the agency shares only one idea, the client spends the entire meeting poking holes in the presentation, looking for flaws or listing reasons why it won't work.

So smart agencies share multiple directions—not ten or fifteen but two or three—and let the client pick which one they like the best. Increasing buy-in for whichever route is selected.

Try to convince people to do something, and they spend a lot of time counterarguing. Thinking about all the various reasons why it's a bad idea or why something else would be better. Why they *don't* want to do what was suggested.

But give people multiple options, and suddenly things shift.

Rather than thinking about what is wrong with whatever was suggested, they think about which one is better. Rather than poking holes in whatever was raised, they think about which of the options is best for them. And because they've been participating, they're much more likely to go along with one of them in the end.

A friend of mine used to gripe about how his wife asked his opinion but then shot down his suggestions. She'd ask, "Where do you want to go to dinner?" or "What do you feel like doing this weekend?" But if he responded, "Mexican sounds good" or "Let's check out that festival that's happening on Sunday," she'd always say no: "We just had Mexican last week" or "I think it'll be too hot on Sunday to be outside all day."

It would drive him nuts. "Why does she ask me what I want, just so she can say no?" he would complain. "Is she using me like some perverse sounding board?"

Then he tried a slightly different tack. Rather than suggesting one thing, he suggested two. Rather than just suggesting Mexican, he would say either Mexican or sushi sounded good. Rather than suggesting the festival, he'd say they could go to the festival or binge-watch one of their favorite shows. Rather than giving her one option, he gave her a menu.

And suddenly she stopped arguing. She never liked both options he suggested, and she'd still come up with some reason why one option was less than ideal, but at least she'd pick one.

Because now that option wasn't just his suggestion that was being foisted on her; it was hers. After all, she had chosen it.[15]

Ask, Don't Tell

Another way to allow for agency is to ask questions rather than make statements.

Nafeez Amin co-owns Sherpa Prep, a test prep and admissions consulting company in Washington, DC. The company runs GMAT and GRE courses, and for more than a decade it has helped hundreds of students get into some of the best graduate programs in the country.

In the early days, though, Nafeez noticed the same problem coming up again and again: students weren't studying enough.

In addition to helping run the company, Nafeez often steps in to teach courses. Most students haven't taken math for several years, and the GMAT doesn't allow test takers to use a calculator, so the first day usually starts with some fundamentals of arithmetic. In addition, Nafeez briefly goes over course logistics.

Encouraging the students to form study plans or tell friends that they are taking the course to encourage accountability.

But when he spoke to students, Nafeez noticed a huge disparity between their expectations and the kind of work that GMAT success would require. Many had no idea what they were in for. Everyone was applying to the same top ten schools, assuming that with just a little effort they would get in. Students didn't understand that top schools often had a 5 percent acceptance rate, even among really qualified applicants.

Many came in thinking about how they had destroyed the SATs or done well on tests in the past. But this was a different pool. It wasn't high school anymore. His students were going against people who'd not only graduated college but had done well enough to think seriously about graduate school. It was a smarter subset. Just doing whatever they'd done before wasn't going to be enough.

When Nafeez asked students how much they planned to study outside of class, the numbers he got back were shockingly low. Five hours a week, most would say; ten tops. Around fifty hours by the end of the course. Nowhere near the two hundred or three hundred hours it usually takes for people to get the scores they need.

But when Nafeez tried to tell students that, all he got back were blank stares. Students either didn't believe him or were so overwhelmed that they dropped out. It came across as pretty harsh on the first day. *Who is this guy to tell me I need to study more?*

Nafeez didn't want to be demotivating, but he wanted students to be realistic. He wanted them to realize that they needed to spend more hours studying outside of class. That it was going to be harder than they anticipated. That it was going to take longer. That it was going to be a process.

So instead of telling students what they needed to do, Nafeez started asking about what they wanted. The next time he taught a class, he started by asking, "Why are you here? What's your goal? Why are you taking the GMAT?"

"I want to get into a top business school," one student said.

"Okay. Do you know what it takes to get into a place like that?" Nafeez asked.

"I've got to get a 720," one student replied. "A 750," said another.

"How'd you get to that number?" Nafeez asked.

Different students chimed in, and the group started having a conversation. Through the process, it came out that around 250,000 people take the GMAT every year. For the top twenty MBA programs, the enrollment is around 10,000. That means lots and lots of people competing for a small number of slots. The students started realizing this was going to be tougher than they thought.

Once this sunk in, Nafeez started guiding the conversation to where he wanted to end up in the first place: how much they needed to study. "So, to get a score that places you in that top percentile, how many hours a week do you think you'll need to study?" Nafeez asked.

Rather than just guessing or throwing out numbers offhand, the students realized they didn't know the answer. So they started asking Nafeez questions. "You've done this for a while, what do you think?" one student asked. "How much does someone like me usually have to study to get a score that will get me into a top program?"

A lightbulb had gone on.

Now when Nafeez threw out the three-hundred-hour number, everyone listened. They did the division and realized that were not going to be able to pack in three hundred or so hours over a ten-week course in five hours a week. They had to adjust their plans. And by the end of the discussion the students ended up tripling the number of hours that they said they were going to study.

Using questions boosted outcomes. Nafeez found that students studied more, got more out of the course, and did better on the test. Not because he told them how much to study, but because he helped them reach that realization on their own.

Questions do a couple things. First, like providing a menu, questions shift the listener's role. Rather than counterarguing or thinking about all the reasons they disagree with a statement, listeners are occupied with a different task: figuring out an answer to the question. How they feel about it or their opinion. Something most people are more than happy to do.

Second, and more importantly, questions increase buy-in. Because while people may not want to follow someone else's lead, they're much more likely to follow their own. The answer to the question isn't just *any* answer; it's *their* answer. And because it's their own personal answer, reflecting their own personal thoughts, beliefs, and preferences, that answer is much more likely to drive them to action.

Warning labels and public health campaigns often provide information, but they do so in the form of declarations: "Junk food makes you fat" or "Drunk driving is murder."

The goal is to be direct, but these approaches often come across as preachy, which generates reactance and activates defensive responses: There's no way junk food makes you fat; I know lots of people who eat at McDonald's and they never seem to gain weight. Or: The ad is exaggerating. My friend drove drunk last week, and no one died. Particularly if people feel strongly about the issue, being too forceful can make them feel threatened and lead the messages to backfire.

The same content, though, can be phrased in terms of a question: Do you think junk food is good for you?

If a person's answer to that question is no, they're now in a tough spot. Because, by asking them to articulate their opinion, the question has encouraged them to put a stake in the ground. To consciously admit that junk food isn't good for them. And once they've done that, it becomes harder to keep eating it.

Questions encourage listeners to *commit to the conclusion*. To behave consistently with whatever answer they gave.

Nafeez asked students what they wanted to achieve, but he didn't pick that question randomly. He picked it knowing that the students' answers would guide them to where he wanted them to go all along.[16]

An executive for a medical device company was having trouble getting salespeople to mentor their subordinates. She sent email after email and had meeting after meeting, encouraging senior employees to guide the younger people they were supposed to be managing.

But pushing wasn't working. Compensation depended on the number of sales made, so managers preferred to spend their time closing deals rather than training others.

Frustrated by the lack of progress, the executive finally asked one of the salespeople, "How did you learn to become such a successful salesman? Where did you learn all those techniques you use today?"

"Oh, I learned from Tim, my old manager who used to work here," the salesman replied.

The executive thought for a moment and then responded, "Well, then how will your team become better salespeople if they don't learn from you?"

Now that salesman is one of the best mentors in the company.

Trying to change company culture or to get a team to go along with a tough reorganization? Rather than taking a predetermined plan and pushing it on people, catalysts do the opposite. They start by asking questions. Visiting with stakeholders, getting their perspectives, and engaging them in the planning process.

This approach has two benefits. First, it gathers information about the problem—not just from survey data or abstract anecdotes but from the real people who are dealing with it every day. Which will make the solution more effective.

Second, and more importantly, when it comes time to roll things out, everyone is more likely to be on board. Because rather than feeling like a declaration that's imposed on them, it'll be a shift they feel they participated in. They've already committed to the conclusion, which will make them more willing to go along with the work to get there—which will speed the change.

Ask, don't tell.*

Highlight a Gap

Giving people a menu, or asking rather than telling, avoids usurping their sense of control. But another route to self-persuasion is

---

* Or alternatively: What do you think is more likely to change someone's mind, asking or telling?

to highlight a gap—a disconnect between someone's thoughts and actions or a disparity between what they might recommend for others versus do themselves.

Can I get a light?

Talk to any smoker, even someone who smokes casually, and they've probably heard this question at least once if not hundreds of times. It's a modest request from one fraternity member to another, like asking someone to hold the elevator. Most people are happy to oblige.

But when smokers in Thailand were stopped on the street and asked this question, their responses were nowhere near as positive. "I'm not giving it to you," said one smoker. "Cigarettes contain poison," responded another. "They drill a hole in your throat for cancer. Aren't you afraid of surgery?" lectured a third. Smoking makes you die faster, leads to lung cancer, and causes a variety of other ailments, they replied.

These weren't public health workers talking. These were every-day smokers who were currently in mid-cigarette themselves. Yet they were inspired to rant about how smoking was a terrible idea.

And they did so because of the person who asked.

Because the person who made the request was a child. A small boy wearing a monkey T-shirt, or a girl in pigtails. Each no more than four feet tall and barely over ten years old. The kids pulled cigarettes from their pockets and politely asked smokers for a light.

After being rejected and often chastised for their request, the kids turned to walk away. But before they did, they handed the smoker a piece of paper. A small note, folded into fourths, almost like a secret passed under the table at school. "You worry about me," it said, "but why not about yourself?"

And at the bottom was a toll-free number smokers could call to kick the habit.*

For more than twenty-five years, the Thai Health Promotion Foundation had promoted this free hotline to help smokers quit. But despite investing millions of dollars in advertising and other persuasive messaging, few people called. Smokers either ignored the campaigns or didn't give the messages much thought. They knew smoking was harmful but weren't doing anything about it.

So, in 2012, the foundation tried reducing roadblocks. They realized that the most convincing speaker wasn't the foundation or celebrities; it was the smokers themselves. To really quit, people had to convince themselves. The foundation designed the Smoking Kid campaign with that insight in mind.

Almost every smoker who received the note from a child paused and threw away their cigarette. But no one threw away the brochure.

With a meager budget of only $5,000 and no media spending at all, the campaign had an enormous impact. Calls to the helpline jumped more than 60 percent. A video filming these interactions went viral, gaining more than 5 million views in barely more than a week. Even months later, calls to the helpline remained up by almost a third. Many called it the most effective anti-smoking ad ever.

The Smoking Kid campaign worked because it highlighted a gap, a disconnect between what smokers were suggesting to others (kids) and what they were doing themselves.

---

* See jonahberger.com/videos for a video of the campaign.

People strive for internal consistency. They want their attitudes, beliefs, and behaviors to align. Someone who says they care about the environment tries to reduce their carbon footprint. Someone who preaches the virtues of honesty tries not to tell lies.

Consequently, when attitudes and behaviors conflict, people get uncomfortable. And to reduce this discomfort, or what scientists call cognitive dissonance, people take steps to bring things back in line.

Thai smokers faced exactly this discord. They were already smoking, but after telling kids smoking was bad they were stuck. Their attitudes and behavior weren't lining up. To reduce that dissonance, something had to give. Either they started telling kids that smoking isn't so bad after all, or they took a closer look at their own behavior and thought harder about quitting. Which was exactly what they did.

Researchers used a similar idea to get people to save water.[17] California was facing one of its periodic water shortages, and university administrators were desperate to get students to save water by taking shorter showers. Traditional persuasive approaches had some effect, but not enough.

So scientists tried highlighting the gap between attitudes and action. A research assistant stood outside the women's locker room at the University of California, Santa Cruz, and asked students who were about to shower if they would sign a poster encouraging other people to save water. "Take shorter showers," it read. "If I can do it, so can you!"

Support a pro-social cause? Students were more than happy to help.

Then, after signing the poster, students were asked a few brief questions about their own water use, such as "When showering, do you always turn off the water while soaping up or shampooing?" These questions highlighted that their own behavior was less than ideal. That they sometimes wasted water while showering.

Finally, students went to shower. And unbeknown to them, a second research assistant unobtrusively recorded how long they left the water on. (To make sure the students didn't realize they were being timed, the assistant pretended to shower in another stall while timing things using a waterproof stopwatch.)

Highlighting the gap between students' attitudes and actions drastically reduced water use. They shortened their showers by more than a minute, or more than 25 percent. And they were twice as likely to turn off the shower while shampooing or soaping up.

Reminding students that they didn't always practice what they preached encouraged them to change their practices.

This approach works even when the dissonance isn't as obvious.

People who deny climate change exists are unlikely to want polluted air for their kids. Employees who are wedded to old, inefficient processes are unlikely to recommend the same approach to new hires. There's a disconnect between what people are saying or doing and what they would want or recommend for others.

Take a project that's not working out, or a division that is consistently losing money. It really should be killed off, but some people are wedded to it. "Give it a chance," they say. "Give it more time." Inertia kicks in and they can't seem to let go, even though they should.

Rather than trying to convince them to kill it, take a different tack. Shift the reference point.

If they were starting from scratch today, given what they know now, would they suggest starting the project? If a new CEO were hired, would they suggest keeping the division? If not, why should we?

Highlighting such dissonance, and bringing it to the fore, encourages people not only to see the discord but also to work to resolve it.

Start with Understanding

The final way catalysts allow for autonomy goes back, as surprising as it may seem, to the approach used by hostage negotiators like Greg Vecchi.

Over the last few decades, negotiators have relied on a simple stairway model. Whether trying to convince an international terrorist to let hostages go or to change someone's mind about committing suicide, a basic set of steps consistently works.

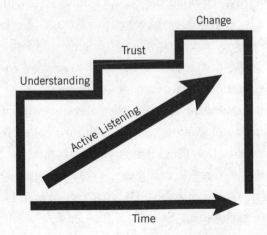

The first step isn't influence or persuasion. Like most people trying to change minds, novice negotiators want to be direct, saying, "Let the hostages go now or we'll shoot!" Immediately jumping to the outcome they want to achieve.

Not surprisingly, tactics like this don't work. They come across as blunt and overly aggressive, and often lead conflicts to escalate. Because starting by trying to influence someone makes it all about you. It's not about other people, and their wants and motivations; it's about you and what you want.

Before people will change, they have to be willing to listen. They have to trust the person they're communicating with. And until that happens, no amount of persuasion is going to work.

Think about why word of mouth is more persuasive than advertising. If an advertisement says a new restaurant is good, people don't usually believe it. Because they don't think they can trust what the ad is saying.

But if their friend says they'll love the homemade tagliatelle, they're much more likely to give it a shot. Why? Because that friend has earned permission. They've known the friend long enough to assume she has their best interests at heart.

Consequently, seasoned negotiators don't start with what *they* want; they start with *whom* they want to change. Working to gain insight into where that person is coming from. Comprehending and appreciating that person's situation, feelings, and motives, and showing them that someone else understands.

People in a crisis can feel like they have no support. They're angry and upset and want to be heard. But it's gotten to this crisis point because they don't feel like anyone is listening.

Consequently, Greg Vecchi starts every negotiation the same way: "Hi, I'm Greg with the FBI. Are you okay?" He says that whether the person is a five-year-old child or a fifty-year-old bank robber, a suicidal mom or a murderer. That's his opening line.

It's not something formal, like "This is Special Agent Vecchi," and it's certainly not "come out with your hands up or we're going to take you out." That doesn't exactly build trust.

Instead, Greg starts by building a bridge. By letting the person talk, without judgment and without inserting himself, he starts forming a relationship. Making the person feel like they are a true stakeholder in the interaction. By asking the right questions, he shows that he's listening, and that he cares.

In addition to showing compassion and understanding, the questions also help gather valuable information. So-called tactical empathy helps negotiators understand what the underlying issue really is: why a suspect is upset or what they need. By staying in the person's frame and making it about them, smart negotiators both build connection and lay the groundwork for influence.

This is often the hardest thing for inexperienced negotiators to do. To listen to someone else and put themselves in that person's shoes rather than move directly toward resolution. But resolution can only be achieved after building the foundation to get there.

Because when people feel like someone is truly listening and cares about their well-being, a sense of trust begins to form.

Greg talks about it as becoming their helper. Their advocate or means to get what they want. "It sounds like you're hungry. Let me get you some food." "You want a getaway car? What type of car do you want?" He becomes the intermediary, their partner. From the beginning he establishes that he is there to help them and that they are a team.

This even shows up in the language Greg uses. "*You and I* are going to work this out." "*We've* got to keep working *together*, because *we* don't want it taken out of *our* hands, right?" Inclusive pronouns create a world where Greg is going to help and protect the person as much as he can, but the person needs to help him do that. It's hard for people to remain angry at someone trying to help them.

Only then, after he's built understanding and established trust, does Greg try to create change. He's got to get the person to the place where they are willing to listen to his suggestions and direction.

And even when he gets to that place, he makes sure to solve things from their perspective. Got a would-be bank robber holed up with two hostages? Telling them to come out so they can be taken into custody probably isn't going to work. That's what Greg wants them to do, but the robber doesn't want to go to jail.

What's more effective is getting the robber to feel that the solution was *their* idea. Getting them to convince themselves. Vecchi uses the bank robber's own words and mirrors them back to make it fit what he wants. Encouraging the bank robber to come to his own conclusion that coming out with his hands up is the best way to go.

This doesn't just mean doing whatever the bank robber wants. Because the robber's first preference would be to escape with all the money, never to be heard from again. To get off scot-free. And Greg can't let that happen.

Instead, what is so powerful about Greg's approach is that he gets the bank robber to comply, not by *telling* them what to do, but by making them feel like Greg is looking out for them. In this way Greg helps the bank robber get to the place Greg wanted to go all along. Where the best way for the robber to achieve their own goals is to come out with their hands up.

Several years ago Greg was negotiating with a father (call him John) who was threatening to commit suicide. John was despondent. He'd lost his job, couldn't find another one, and was worried about being able to provide for his family. The only way he could see to help them was to kill himself. He had a large life insurance policy, and if he died, he hoped the money would help take care of them.

In situations like this, people's first reaction is to be direct. The insurance company is not going to pay out if John commits suicide, so you should tell him, right?

But that's not in John's frame. That's not understanding where he's coming from. And if you start trying to be rational with him and talk from your perspective rather than his, he's probably going to kill himself.

So Greg started with John. He introduced himself, asked John if he was okay, and began to work to understand what his underlying issues were. "I worked for this guy for twenty years," John says, "and I was fired and now I have no income. The bank owns everything. I've got to take care of my family, and so this is what I'm going to do. I've got good insurance money. No one needs me."

"Tell me about your family," Greg says, turning into Mr. Helper, trying to learn about John because he cares about him.

"Oh, well, I've got a wife and two great kids," says John.

And because he put emphasis on the kids, Greg picks that positive subject as the one to explore further. "Well, tell me about your kids."

"Well, yeah. I've got—they're two boys," said John.

"They're two boys? Really?" said Greg, paraphrasing and mirroring.

"Yeah," replied John.

"Well, sounds like you love them," said Greg, labeling the emotions. "Sounds like you really love them."

"Well, yeah, of course I do," said John.

"Seems to me you're a really, really great dad who's trying to do the right thing." said Greg.

"Well, yeah, of course I am, right?" replied John.

Greg gets John to start talking about his kids and their relationship. How John wants them to be good boys and respect women. How John takes them out fishing and teaches them life skills. How much his kids love spending time with him.

And after they've been talking for a while and John shares all this information, Greg comes back with "Well, gee, John. It seems to me that if you kill yourself today, your boys are going to lose their best friend."

And then: silence.

Vecchi says nothing and just lets what he said sink in.

Because Vecchi just put a dilemma in John's head. Not by telling him what to do, or by pushing, but by listening and reframing John's own words. And because he's developed a relationship with John, and helped him, and done it all without judgment, it's tough not to listen.

Now John's not going to kill himself. Because suicide no longer seems like a viable option.

Trying to prevent someone from committing suicide is an extremely tough situation. Hopefully it's one that most of us will never have to be in.

But the approach Greg used is equally effective in a range of daily encounters. From conversations with a supplier to arguments with a spouse.

Rather than trying to persuade, start by understanding. Why is the supplier's price higher than desired? Perhaps their costs have gone up. What about dirty dishes in the sink makes your spouse so upset? Maybe it's the dishes themselves, but maybe it's a constant reminder of a larger, unresolved issue.

When people feel understood and cared about, trust develops. The supplier realizes the goal is a long-term partnership and not just a money grab. The spouse realizes that sometimes dirty dishes are just dirty dishes. And along the way, together, you find a path to a solution.*

It's like weeding a garden. The quickest approach is grab the top of the weed, rip it out of the ground, and move on to the next one.

But while that is a fast way to make things look better, it's a terrible long-term solution. Because if only the top of the weed is removed, it just grows back. Soon. What seems like a shortcut ends up taking more time.

To truly get rid of weeds, or change minds, find the root. Discover whatever needs and motivations are driving behavior in the first place. Find the root and the rest will follow.

---

* Starting with understanding also diffuses anti-persuasion radar by making sure the other side gets a chance to say their piece. In most negotiations, arguments, or discussions, people spend a lot of time thinking about what they are going to say next. Why what you said was wrong, or a justification for why their side is right. Which means that, instead of focusing on what you're saying, they're thinking about counterarguments. Rather than really hearing what you have to say, they're monitoring the conversation, looking for spots to get their points in. Giving them a chance to explain themselves increases the chance that they'll then listen when you start speaking.

For more tactics negotiators use to change minds,
see the Active Listening appendix.

Repurposing Reactance

When people feel like someone is pushing or trying to convince them, they often push back, digging in their heels and resisting.

To change minds, then, we need to stop trying to persuade, and encourage people to persuade themselves. Like savvy parents, we need to provide a menu or guided choices that allow people to pick their path to the desired outcome. Like Nafeez Amin, we need to ask, don't tell; using questions to encourage people to commit to the conclusion and see how what we want is actually the best way for them to reach an outcome they care about. Like the Thai Health Promotion Foundation, we need to highlight a gap or a disconnect between what people might recommend for others versus do themselves. And, like Greg Vecchi, we need to start with understanding, building trust by finding the root.

No one likes feeling someone is trying to influence them. After all, when's the last time you changed your mind because someone told you to?

How to Change an Extremist's Mind

So far, we've shown how reducing reactance can help catalyze change in a variety of situations. From getting teens to stop smoking to inspiring salespeople to be better mentors; and from getting spouses to agree to encouraging criminals to come out with their hands up.

But can this concept really be used to change *anyone's* mind?

It was a sunny Sunday morning in June when the phone rang. Michael and Julie Weisser were at their kitchen table. They had only been in their new home a few days and the corners of the large eat-in kitchen were still filled with half-unloaded cardboard boxes.

Michael was closest to the phone, so he walked over and picked up the receiver. "Hello," he said.

A man's voice on the other end came through loudly with deep hatefulness: "You will be sorry you ever moved to 5810 Randolph Street, Jew boy."

And then the line went dead.[18]

The Weissers had come to Lincoln, Nebraska, seeking opportunity. Congregation B'nai Jeshurun, the oldest congregation in the city, was looking for a new spiritual leader, and after serving in various cantor and rabbinical roles across the United States, Michael was looking for a new challenge.

Lincoln was mostly a Christian evangelical community and of the more than 200,000 residents, only a few hundred identified as Jewish. Typical attendance at the reform congregation was often fewer than a dozen people, and Michael worked hard to grow attendance.

Two and a half years after Michael arrived, membership in the temple had grown to one hundred families, and there was new energy under Michael's leadership.

Then, out of the blue, the ominous phone call.

How did this person know their address? Let alone the fact that they were Jewish? They were most afraid for their kids, who stayed home by themselves after school until Michael and Julie got home from work.

A couple days later, things got worse.

Julie had just returned from a long day at the office and walked down the driveway to get the mail. In between the usual bills and letters there was a thick brown envelope addressed to Rabbi Michael Weisser.

When she took it inside to open it, out poured a stack of papers. Flyers and brochures, each one more racist and terrible than the next. Images of Jews with stereotypically huge hooked noses and pictures of black people with gorilla heads. Nazi pamphlets championing the Holocaust and quotes from "authorities" that "proved" the racial inferiority of nonwhites.

On top of it all was a small card. It read: "The KKK is watching you, scum."

———————

The Weissers had experienced racism before. When one of their sons dated an African American girl back in Memphis, someone once called him a "race traitor." Another time someone came up to their daughter at school and yelled that she was a "Christ killer."

But nothing had been as scary as this.

The response from the police was unambiguous. "Let's put it this way," one officer said. "If the person behind this package is the local head of the KKK—which we suspect it is—he's dangerous. We know he makes explosives."

The man's name was Larry Trapp. When it came to white supremacists in the area, Trapp was the leader. A grand dragon of the White Knights of the Ku Klux Klan, Trapp was responsible for the entire state. His goal was nothing less than to "build Nebraska into one of the foremost Klan enclaves in the country."

Trapp loved violence and stockpiled machine guns and automatic weapons. He worked to incite violence throughout the region, which included threatening a local Vietnamese refugee assistance center, then having his goons break in at night and torch the place.

The Weissers didn't know what to do. They installed deadbolts on the doors and made sure to lock everything before going out. They felt nervous when cars drove slowly by the house, and the kids took different routes home from school every day to avoid being targeted. Michael and Julie hated feeling intimidated, but they didn't see any other option.

Julie started trying to pick up information about Larry Trapp. She worked at a local doctor's office, and it turned out that Trapp was well-known in the local medical community. He had been diabetic as a child, but the disease had long gone untreated, leaving him nearly blind. The illness had also severely inhibited blood flow to his legs, which led to some of his toes being amputated and eventually both of his legs.

Confined to a wheelchair, Trapp jumped from doctor to doctor, berating the staff as he went. He was noncompliant and verbally abusive, and one staffing agency even refused to send help to his apartment because he'd pulled a gun on one of their nurses.

Julie was able to find out Trapp's home address, and one day, while driving home, she found herself making a detour. She drove down the street until she was looking at Trapp's unremarkably plain brown one-story apartment building. Why was he doing these terrible things? she wondered. Was he crazy? Lonely? Why was he filled with so much hate?

She started driving by the address again and again. Feeling frustrated, she flipped through the Bible and came across a verse that described Trapp perfectly: "A worthless person, a wicked man, goes about with crooked speech . . . with perverted heart devises evil, continually sowing discord; therefore, calamity will come upon him suddenly; in a moment he will be broken beyond healing" (Proverbs 6:12–15).

Inspired by what she read, she considered sending Trapp a letter, sharing the proverb with him. Michael wasn't sure it was such a good idea. Even if Julie wanted to do that, he said, she should do it anonymously. Her friends said the same thing. "You don't know the mind-set of this person. He's crazy. He's sick in the head! You don't know how he'll react."

Weeks later, Trapp's skinheads sponsored a program on local public access television. The White Aryan resistance had put together a video showing Nazis, Klansmen, and similar groups strutting around, spewing hate and white supremacy. The community access coordinator said the station couldn't simply refuse a show because of its content. So it went on the air.

Michael found the program revolting. He was disgusted that Larry Trapp could get away with making so many people afraid. He couldn't hold back anymore. He decided he would call Trapp.

Michael found Trapp's number and dialed it. No one answered, but the answering machine spewed a vicious tirade.

Michael didn't leave a message, but after the recording ended, he called back. *At least nobody else can get through to listen to this crap,* he thought.

Soon he was calling back regularly. Eventually Michael decided to leave a message. He was angry, and part of him wanted to yell at Larry, to threaten him with all the force he could muster. But Michael was also a man of faith, so he simply said: "Larry, you better think about all this hatred you're spreading, because one day you're going to have to answer to God for all this hatred, and it's not going to be easy."

Before long, whenever he had a free moment, Michael was calling Larry's number and leaving short messages. "Why do you hate me? You don't even know me, so how can you hate me?" Another time he said: "Larry, do you know the very first laws that Hitler's Nazis passed were against people like yourself who had no legs? . . . Do you realize you would have been among the first to die under Hitler? Why do you love Nazis so much?"

Some of the messages were direct and some were more oblique. But all of them were powerful in one way or another. "Larry, there's a lot of love out there. You're not getting any of it. Don't you want some?"

Michael called the messages "love notes."

————————

While he was receiving these messages, Larry's own world was starting to shift. He was implicated in a string of nighttime arson attacks. A former neighbor pressed charges for threatening and insulting messages Trapp had left him. A fellow Klansman whom Trapp knew and respected was robbed and killed by two other Klansmen. His health started to decline further.

To make things worse, the messages being left on his machine were starting to disturb him a great deal. He never knew when he'd get another call. The voice was always warm, melodic, and filled with happiness and joy.

The messages made Trapp angry. Who did this caller think he was anyway? Trapp had to put a stop to them.

So the next time the caller rang and began to speak, Larry grabbed the phone. "What the fuck d'ya want?" he said harshly. "Why the fuck are you harassing me? Stop harassing me!"

"I don't want to harass you, Larry, I just want to talk to you."

"You *are* harassing me. What do you want? Make it quick."

Michael paused for a moment. "Well, I was thinking you might need a hand with something," Michael said, "and I wondered if I could help. I know you're in a wheelchair and I thought maybe I could take you to the grocery store or something."

Larry was taken aback. He didn't know what to say.

The line was silent.

Then Larry slowly cleared his throat, and for the first time his voice sounded different. It sounded less filled with hatred. Less hardened.

"That's nice of you, but I've got that covered. Thanks anyway. But don't call this number anymore. It's my business phone."

Late one Saturday night the Weissers were at home, talking about what movie they should see, when the phone rang. The caller asked for "the rabbi," and when Michael picked up the line, he immediately knew the voice on the other end.

"I want to get out," Larry said, "but I don't know how."

"Would you like some help?" asked Michael.

"I don't know what to say," Larry said. "I'm feeling confused and kind of sick. I think this is making me sick."

Michael offered to come over and Larry demurred. Michael asked if Larry was hungry and finally Larry gave in. Michael offered to pick up some food and Larry gave them his apartment number.

When Trapp opened the door and Michael shook his hand, Larry winced like he had been hit with a jolt of electricity and broke into tears. Trapp looked down at the swastika rings on his fingers and couldn't bear to wear them anymore. As he handed them to Michael he said, "They stand for all the hatred in my life. Will you take them away?"

Larry began to sob more loudly. "I'm sorry," he said, "so sorry for the things I've done." Michael and Julie put their arms around him and told him that everything would be okay.

On November 16, 1991, Trapp formally resigned from the Ku Klux Klan. Next he turned to apologizing to all the people he had hurt. All the individuals he had threatened. He sent a letter to the news media apologizing for "the abusive language and racial epithets that I have used towards various races and individuals in the state of Nebraska."

He cleaned out all the racist detritus that had built up in his home and tried to start again.

His relationship with Michael and Julie blossomed into a close friendship.

That New Year's Eve, Trapp found out that his kidneys were failing and that he had less than a year to live. The Weissers invited him to move in with them and he agreed. They converted their living room into a bedroom, and Julie quit her job to tend to Larry's deteriorating health.

Eventually, Larry converted to Judaism. He did so at Michael's synagogue, the very one that he had at one point planned to blow up. A little over three months later he died in the Weissers' home.

Larry Trapp had spent his entire childhood hiding from his abusive father. Whether consciously or not, he spent much of his adult life trying to please that same father, who was also an avowed racist. In some strange way, emulating the thing that had hurt him the most gave Larry the strength he needed to go on. Until one day someone showed him another option.

Michael wasn't the first person who tried to encourage Larry to change. The cops dragged Trapp down to the police station time and time again.

Back then, policing was all about punishment: "We've got to stop this behavior any way we can." But the police never really stopped to think about why the problem was there in the first place. What was this guy dealing with that would make him act this way?

Decades ago, when Michael Weisser initially interviewed for the position with the temple board of directors, he spoke about the importance of core religious principles: love, tolerance, and nonharmful behavior. "'Love your neighbor as yourself!' We're not talking about our neighbor who is the same as we are. No, we're talking about the neighbor who is *different* from us."

Now, when asked why Larry changed his mind, Michael points to a similar idea.

No amount of pushing was going to get Larry to give up the Klan. But by extending Larry an olive branch and telling him that someone cared, Michael showed him that there was something more powerful than hate.

"Lead a horse to water, but you can't make him drink," Michael said. "But if they're thirsty, they'll drink. And so that's the way it was with Larry."

Larry didn't change because Michael told him to. He changed because he came to that conclusion on his own terms. But Michael didn't just stand on the sidelines. He reduced reactance, guiding Larry down a path Larry could explore himself.

"Kind of walking by his side like those footprints in the sand," said Michael. "Not pushing him one way or the other but walking in a certain direction. He was coming along for the ride at first and then he took the lead for himself. And if I was the catalyst for that, then I think I did a good thing."

As Trapp himself said: "I was one of the most hardcase white activists in the U.S. If I can have that change of mind or change of heart, anybody can."

Michael changed Larry's mind by reducing reactance. Rather than telling Larry what he should do, Michael opened up a line of communication and encouraged Larry to convince himself.

Reactance, though, isn't the only barrier to change. Because even when someone's anti-persuasion radar isn't on red alert, they often seem attached to what they're already doing.

As we'll discuss in chapter 4, "Uncertainty," people often have "neophobia": they undervalue or avoid new things, because change often involves uncertainty. It's unclear whether the new thing will be good or not.

But in addition to undervaluing new things, people also overvalue what they have already. The products and services they're using, ideas and attitudes they're holding, or programs and initiatives they're participating in. And to understand why, we have to appreciate the power of endowment.

2. Endowment

A few years ago I had a problem with my phone. I'd had it for almost six years and loved it. It had all the features I wanted, fit nicely in my pocket, and was generally a great device.

But it was running out of memory. All the accumulated pictures and videos, combined with increasing app sizes, had consumed the available space.

Initially, this was no big deal. There were songs I never listened to and apps I never used, so I got rid of them.

Soon, though, unused files became harder to find. Every time I wanted to take a new photo, I had to start by deleting an old one. Which did I care more about: Aunt Jan and her birthday or the puppy's first day in the snow?

Friends suggested I look into a new phone, so I did. The newer models had a faster processor, an extra camera, and lots of additional space. But they were also almost 20 percent longer than my old phone and wider as well. It was hard to hold one and type with the same hand and even harder to fit the thing in my pocket.

Was size the most important attribute? No. In fact, if you had asked me ahead of time, I probably wouldn't have even thought of it myself. But seeing it in person was enough to make me think twice about getting the new model.

I didn't want a *different* phone; I wanted the same phone I already had, just updated slightly. Apple was supposed to release a smaller-footprint version eventually, so why not give it a few more months?

But as I waited, my old phone went into a slow and steady death spiral.

First, an ominous red dot appeared in the settings app. Apple had pushed a new operating system, but I was out of space.

Then the airline apps asked to be updated. But they required the new operating system. That meant no more mobile boarding passes and one more thing to think about every week when I traveled. Like a prop plane whose engines slowly fail one by one, different features of my phone gradually disengaged.

Through all of this, I waited. Through one indignity after another, I stuck by my old phone.

Finally, after almost missing a flight because I hadn't printed a boarding pass, I caved. I broke down, called my phone company, and ordered a new phone.

One would think this was the end of the story. That the new phone would arrive, I'd tear open the package, and happily start using it.

But that wasn't what happened.

Because even after the phone arrived, I still didn't use it. I was so attached to my old phone that I didn't open the new one for more than three months. Weeks went by as I held on to the old technology. All the while, my old phone was becoming more and more obsolete.

You might find this story funny. Ridiculous, even. But it's more common than you might think.

New things are often better. Phones are faster and have more memory. Services are more comprehensive and deliver better results. Management strategies are more current and effective. People should switch.

But they don't.

Even though the new thing is technically better, people still cling to the old. They follow the same processes and maintain the same courses of action.

And while it's easy to attribute this to nostalgia, something subtler is at play.

Of Mugs and Men

Think about the last time your power went out. Using your phone as a flashlight but worrying it would run out of juice. Having to reset all the clocks once the outage ended. And, if the outage was particularly long, tossing all the spoiled food in the fridge. All in all, not a lot of fun.

No one likes power outages, but Pacific Gas and Electric Company—or PG&E, as its most commonly called—wanted to understand exactly how much consumers disliked them. PG&E works to balance reliability and cost. They could invest in more preventive measures, but that would make the service more expensive. Or they could cut rates, but reliability would likely suffer.

So which did customers prefer, greater reliability or lower cost?

To find out, researchers surveyed more than 1,300 consumers and asked them which of six power plans they preferred.[1] Some plans were more expensive but promised fewer and shorter outages, while other plans were cheaper but involved more frequent, longer outages.

Not surprisingly, when most customers were asked, few picked the plan with lots of power outages. It meant a four-hour outage at least once a month: more time sitting in the dark or worrying about the food in the fridge going bad. Most customers currently experienced around three outages a year, so they said they'd need a monthly discount of at least $20 to move to a service that bad.

But one group of people liked the higher power outage plan a lot. Even though it meant worse service.

Why would they prefer less reliable service? Were they older or more price sensitive, which might lead them to prefer cheaper service, even if it was less reliable?

No, the only difference was the status quo. What they were getting already. A small group of people were already experiencing lots of power outages—as many as fifteen a year of four hours each—so they picked a plan that was similar to what they knew, even though to most people it seemed like a terrible option.[2]

The status quo bias is everywhere. People tend to eat the same foods they've always eaten, buy the same brands they've always bought, and donate to the same causes they've always supported.

Take someone who's just had heart bypass surgery or had an angioplasty to widen obstructed arteries. Afterward they're told, often multiple times by multiple doctors, to change their diets and lifestyles. But only around 10 percent actually do.[3]

Change is hard, because people tend to overvalue what they have: what they already own or are already doing.

Consider this ceramic coffee mug:

It's off-white, has a nice strong handle, and would be good for drinking any hot beverage of your choice. How much would you be willing to pay for such a mug? What's the most you would pay to purchase it?

When asked a similar question, people said they would pay a little less than $3 on average. It was a nice mug, fine enough, but nothing too valuable.

A different group was asked a slightly different question. They were shown the same mug, but rather than being asked about their willingness to buy the mug, they took a *seller's* perspective. They were given a mug and asked the lowest amount they would be willing to *accept* to *sell* it.

The buying and selling amounts should be the same. After all, it's the same coffee mug, so whether people are buying or selling it, they should have the same valuation.

But they didn't. Sellers, on average, wanted more than twice as much to part with the mug. Or a little over $7.

Why?

Well, it's not just that people are capitalists and want to buy low and sell high. It turns out that once we have something, once we're endowed with it, we start to become attached to it. And consequently we value it more.

This so-called endowment effect happens all the time.[4] Duke University students were willing to pay around $200 for Final Four tickets, but students who already had tickets wanted more than $2,000 to sell them. Memorabilia dealers value the same baseball card more if they own it than if they don't. And whether considering time, intellectual property, or a host of other things, people demand more to give them up than acquire them. Ownership even increases the perceived value of beliefs and ideas. When something is *ours*, we value it more.

In fact, the longer people do or own something, the more they value it.[5] The longer homeowners have lived in a home, for example, the higher they value it over the market price. The more they become attached to it, the harder it becomes to give it up.[6]

Loss Aversion

Every change has upsides and downsides. A new phone has better battery life but a bigger footprint. A new power plan has fewer outages but costs more. New software saves money but has to be integrated with the old system and takes a while to learn.

It turns out that these advantages and disadvantages aren't weighted equally.

Imagine I offered you a chance to win $100 on a coin flip. If it lands heads, you win a hundred dollars; and if it lands tails, you lose a hundred. Would you take that bet?

If you're like most people, you'd probably say no. Sure, there's the chance of winning $100, but there's an equal chance of losing $100, so the potential gain doesn't seem worth the risk. Might as well stay put and do nothing.

Classical economics would generally agree. Calculate the expected value, or the sum of all possible outcomes multiplied by their probability of occurrence, and the resulting number is zero. A 50 percent chance of winning $100 means plus $50, and a 50 percent chance of losing $100 means minus $50, so adding them together nets zero. Consequently, people should be indifferent between taking the bet or not. Given the effort of participating, one could even say the expected value is slightly negative, so most people would decline.

But imagine sweetening the deal just a tiny bit. Rather than winning $100 on heads, make it $102. Same potential downside but a larger potential upside.

Standard economics would say you should take that bet. The expected value is (50% × $102) + (50% × –$100) = $51 – $50 = $1. A dollar isn't huge, but play that gamble 100 times and, on average, you should win $100, so expected value would say go for it.

But would you? Would you be willing to risk $100 for the chance to win $102?

Probably not. In fact, I'd probably have to increase the upside significantly to get more than a couple of takers.

Because losses loom larger than gains. When deciding whether to take a bet, buy a new phone, or make any change at all, potential disadvantages are weighed more heavily than potential advantages. Losing $100 feels worse than winning $100. Losing $100 even feels worse than winning $110.

In fact, research suggests that the potential gains of doing something have to be 2.6 times larger than the potential losses to get people to take action. Chance of losing $100? The potential win has to be at least $260 before most people will take that bet.[7]

Whenever people think about changing, they compare things to their current state. The status quo. And if the potential gains barely outweigh the potential losses, they don't budge.

To get people to change, the advantages have to be at least twice as good as the disadvantages. New software can't be just a little better; it has to be *a lot* better. A new approach can't just be slightly more effective; it has to be *significantly* more effective. If people have to give up something they like or lose things they value, the benefit (e.g., boosted efficiency, decreased cost, or some other positive change) has to be at least twice as big to make up for it.*

And while the advantages of new things are often salient, potential change agents often ignore the disadvantages or costs.

Take something like buying a new laptop. The monetary costs are easy to see, but there are several less obvious costs. The time required to read reviews, compare attributes, and figure out which potential alternative is best. The effort to order the new

---

* Two aspects are important to note. First, the new thing doesn't have to be twice as good as the old one; the upside (i.e., benefits or gains) just has to be twice as large as any downsides (i.e., costs or losses). For example, a new service doesn't need to be twice as fast as the old one, but the increase in speed or other benefit needs to be at least twice as large as any monetary cost to acquire it, time spent learning how to use it, etc. Second, *perceived* gains and losses are what matter: the service may be twice as fast, but if the customer doesn't care about speed, it doesn't matter. Similarly, if some consumers actually like a larger phone, then the increased size wouldn't be a loss; it would actually be a gain. Loss aversion doesn't operate on attributes but on changes. If a new car is perceived to have all the benefits of the old one, there is no loss, even if some of the attributes differ. Truly understanding someone's needs and values helps determine whether a particular change will be *perceived* as a gain or loss.

device, get everything set up, and learn a new layout and system. This doesn't even include the potential cost of regret for making the wrong choice.

These different aspects can all be described as *switching costs*. The financial, psychological, or procedural (e.g., time and effort) impediments to switching products and services, but also suppliers, doctors, payment systems, routes to work, or basically anything.

There are switching costs to changing grocery stores (figuring out where things are), tennis partners (figuring out who will do what), offices (remembering who sits where and where things go), and strategies (overruling past habits).

All this makes it easier to just stick with what was done before, even if it isn't perfect.

And that's exactly what happened with me and my phone. Sure, the new model was technologically better. It was faster and sharper and all those other things that new technology often is.

But were the benefits twice as good as the costs of switching? Not really.

Switching to the new version required moving beyond what I had already. Giving up the smaller footprint phone that I knew and loved. And that potential loss, the various downsides, made it hard to switch.

So how do we ease endowment?

Two key ways are to (1) surface the cost of inaction, and (2) burn the ships.

Surface the Cost of Inaction

As part of the introductory marketing course at the Wharton School, MBA students often read a well-known case study about a fictitious beer brewing company called Mountain Man.[8] The family-owned business has been making one beer, Mountain Man Lager, for more than eighty years. They have a strong reputation for quality throughout the Midwest and an extremely loyal customer base of working-class males—guys who drink the beer at the bar on their way home from a tough day of work.

In the early 2000s, though, the company's leadership was struggling with how to respond to changing consumer preferences. Light-beer sales were growing and fewer people were drinking lager, so for the first time in history, company sales were declining. Not by a lot, but around 2 percent a year.

Management was considering introducing a light beer but worried it would alienate current customers. If yuppies who like light beer started drinking the brand, their core customers—coal miners and guys in camouflage—might move on to something else.

The entire case rests on whether introducing a light beer will kill the core brand. The MBAs estimate potential new light-beer sales, calculate how that might hurt existing lager sales, and come to a decision about how damaging the introduction might be.

Everyone is worried about the risk of doing something new. Will introducing a light beer lead to a 5 percent reduction in lager sales or a 20 percent drop? How much will the introduction erode brand equity, or cause those core consumers to stop buying the brand?

But while the MBAs spend a lot of time thinking about the potential dangers of making a change, they tend to spend less time thinking about something equally important: The risks of doing nothing.

Because while doing the same thing the company has done for eighty years feels safer than doing something new, that's not necessarily the case. Sales are declining. So doing nothing doesn't mean nothing bad happens; it means the company slowly but surely disappears into oblivion.

Which do you think causes more pain? A severe injury, like breaking a finger or shattering a kneecap, or a milder one, like spraining a finger or a trick knee?

As people age, they tend to pick up small, niggling injuries here and there. A sprained finger, jammed through playing basketball or football, that doesn't bend all the way closed. A trick knee, damaged through tennis or daily activities, that buckles every once in a while. A soreness in the shoulder or back that never seems to go away.

These injuries aren't that severe. Sure, they flare up once in a while, and they're a little painful when they do, but often they end up being an annoyance more than anything else. A minor issue rather than a major one.

And while these minor issues aren't ideal, they seem much better than more severe ones. Things like breaking a leg, having a heart attack, or shattering a kneecap.

Indeed, ask people which they'd prefer, and it's not even a question. A trick knee might be annoying, but a shattered kneecap is horrible. It requires invasive surgery and months of arduous rehab; wearing a cast and limiting your range of motion until things heal. If a trick knee is a couple of flies buzzing around your house, a shattered kneecap is the place being infested with cockroaches.

But a closer look reveals something interesting. Recovery may paradoxically be faster from severe injuries than mild ones because of how people respond when those injuries occur.

When a severe injury occurs, people take active steps to speed recovery. They consult physicians, undergo surgeries, and take medicines. They talk to physical therapists, devise treatments, and sketch out rehabilitation plans. All in an effort to get better fast.

But lesser injuries tend not to marshal the same resources. Of course, people might take a couple ibuprofen or put some ice on their sprained finger when they get home, but they're much less likely to pull together a treatment plan.

And even if they do put together a plan, they're less likely to follow it. People *should* take two ibuprofen every morning and do the ten minutes of physical therapy to loosen things up, but who has time to do that every day before work? Soon the exercise sheet ends up under a pile of papers and the ibuprofen bottle is back in the medicine cabinet.

In many ways, this differential response makes sense. It takes time and money to consult doctors, see specialists, and generate treatment plans. It takes effort to do physical therapy every morning and remember to take medicine. So, given that these remedies have costs—sometimes substantial ones—people are more likely to seek them out when they have a heart attack than a headache.

But because it isn't significant enough to provoke a major response, the minor stuff never ends up going away.

A trick knee hurts longer than the shattered kneecap because severe injures exceed our pain tolerance and minor ones don't. Serious injuries surpass a critical threshold, triggering major steps to resolve them. But things that aren't painful enough don't generate such significant responses, which means they never end up getting addressed.[9, 10]

If a product or service fails completely, people go out and find a new one. But if it repeatedly underperforms just slightly, there's not as much impetus to change.

When the status quo is terrible, it's easy to get people to

switch. They're willing to change because inertia isn't a viable option. If your place is infested with roaches, you have to call an exterminator; the only question is which one to call.

But when things aren't terrible, or are just okay but not great, it's harder to get people to budge. If the old thing wasn't that bad to begin with, why go to the trouble and incur the costs of doing something new? If it's just a couple of flies in the house, is it really worth the effort to call an exterminator? Maybe the flies will just go away by themselves.

Terrible things get replaced, but mediocre things stick around. Horrible performance generates action, but average performance generates complacency.

To overcome endowment, then, we need to help people realize the cost of doing nothing—that, rather than being safe or costless, sticking with the status quo actually has a downside.

My cousin used to manually enter a sign-off every time he wrote an email. Whether for work or personal use, he would type out "Best, Charles" at the bottom.

When I first heard this, I was flabbergasted. Why not just create an email signature that says "Best, Charles" and then have it automatically added to the end of every note?

"It only takes a couple seconds to type 'Best, Charles,'" he replied. "Besides, I don't know how to set up signatures to be automatic and it'll take time to learn."

For Charles, the status quo seemed sufficient. He knew what he was doing wasn't ideal, but it wasn't bad enough to motivate him to change. What's a few seconds here and there, anyway? It was a headache, not a heart attack.

Besides, the cost of change seemed larger than the benefit.

It would take minutes to set up an automatic signature, and it would only save him a few seconds, so why switch?

After trying again and again to get him to use an email signature, I tried a different approach.

"How many emails do you think you write a week?" I asked.

"I don't know," he replied. "Maybe around four hundred."

"Okay, and how long does it take to manually write each sign-off?" I asked.

"A couple seconds at most," he answered.

"So how much time do you spend each week writing email signatures?"

He paused.

Then he opened the search bar and typed in "how to add an email signature."

Whenever the status quo is okay but not stellar, or mediocre but not terrible, change doesn't seem worth the effort. Because the current state of things doesn't seem that bad.

But surfacing the cost of inaction helps make people realize that sticking with the status quo isn't as costless as it seems.

Sure, manually writing an email sign-off doesn't take that long. Two to three seconds tops. So it doesn't seem worth investing the time to change.

But add those seconds up across four hundred emails a week, and it takes between ten and twenty minutes. Over a year it's more than ten hours. Suddenly an email sign-off seems less like a headache and more like something more severe. Which makes doing something about it seem like a better course of action.

Gloria Barrett is a financial advisor in Southern California. She helps people with wealth management, life insurance, and retirement planning. Some of her younger clients invest more aggressively, with a higher portion of their portfolio in stocks, while older clients invest more cautiously, preferring things like bonds, given their shorter time horizon.

But Gloria had one client whose behavior didn't make any sense. Keith was in his mid-forties and wasn't planning on retiring for another twenty years, but he was behaving way too conservatively. He had over half his money in savings and didn't want to invest it.

Gloria tried giving Keith data showing that the stock market had a higher rate of return. She put together report after report showing that even the most cautious of investments would net more money. But Keith wouldn't budge.

The stock market seemed risky. So while he had invested some, Keith was worried about losing the rest of his assets. Besides, the savings account was generating interest, so while he wasn't making a huge return, the balance increased every year. Not a lot, but enough that keeping the money there seemed good enough.

After one particularly frustrating call, Gloria decided to stop highlighting the potential upside of investing more and frame things differently. Making it more concrete how much money Keith was *losing* by keeping such a stockpile in savings.

Gloria started an imaginary clock on January 1. Then, for every phone call or meeting she had with Keith in the months that followed, she mentioned how much money Keith had lost by sticking to the status quo. First it was only a couple dollars, then a couple hundred, then a couple thousand.

"How can I be losing money?" asked Keith. "I look at my savings account and the balance goes up every time."

"Sure," replied Gloria, "but that doesn't account for inflation.

And compared to what your performance would be, even in a conservative investment, you're losing a good bit."

Keith didn't change right away. He hemmed and hawed and grumbled. But eventually, when the counter reached more than a couple thousand, he broke down and moved a chunk of his money out of savings. The next time they spoke, he switched over most of the rest. Keith still has some money in savings, but it's more commensurate with his time horizon. And his return has increased significantly.

Change is costly. New products cost money and new services take time to learn how to use. New initiatives take effort to develop and new ideas take time to get accustomed to.

And these costs are mostly up-front. You have to pay for a new book before you get to read it, and you have to invest time to learn a new program or platform before you can use it.

The benefits of change, however, tend to take longer to happen. You don't get the enjoyment from the book until it arrives and you start reading, and you often don't see the benefits of a new program until weeks or months after it finally gets up and running.

Not surprisingly, this *cost-benefit timing gap* stymies action. People are impatient. They want the good stuff faster and the bad stuff later. So if changing means costs now and benefits later, they do nothing.

It's like trying to give up sweets. Sure, there's a long-term benefit of losing weight and living healthier, but there's a short-term cost of having to pass up that delicious chocolate cake. And we all know how well that goes.

Consequently, people stick with the status quo. Why incur costs now if you don't have to? Particularly when the status quo doesn't seem that bad.

Business author Jim Collins once said that "good is the enemy of great . . . We don't have great schools, principally because we have good schools. We don't have great government, principally because we have good government. Few people attain great lives, in large part because it is just so easy to settle for a good life."[11]

The same holds for change. When things are good, it's easy to stick to the status quo. Change is costly and requires effort, so as long as things are good enough, the impetus to switch is muted.

But while doing nothing often seems costless, it's often not as costless as it seems. The status quo may be fine—decent, even. But compared to something better, it's worse. And although the difference may seem small, or even inconsequential, added up over time, it becomes quite large.

So, to change minds and ease endowment, catalysts surface the cost of inaction. They make it easier for people to see the difference between what they are doing now and what they could be doing.

And rather than focusing on how much better the new thing is than the old, or the potential gain of action, catalysts do the opposite. They highlight how much people are *losing* by doing nothing.

Because, as loss aversion shows, losses loom larger than gains. Losing $10 feels worse than gaining $10, and becoming less efficient feels worse than becoming more efficient. Seeing how much time or money is being lost is more motivating than seeing how much could have been gained. Making it less likely that people will stick with the status quo.

Framed the right way, even a headache is worth fixing.

Burn the Ships

Surfacing the costs of inaction encourages the realization that doing nothing isn't costless. But when endowment is really strong, sometimes change requires going one step further. And those situations may warrant burning the ships.

As a child, no one would have guessed that Hernán Cortés would grow up to become a famous explorer. Born in Medellín, Spain, to a relatively poor family, he was a small, colicky infant who was often sick. When he was fourteen, his parents encouraged him to study law, but news of Christopher Columbus and his New World discoveries were streaming back to Spain. Cortés couldn't be satisfied living in his small, provincial town and made plans to sail for the Americas.

In 1504, Cortés landed in Hispaniola (what is Haiti and the Dominican Republic today) and spent the next few years establishing himself. He registered as a citizen, became a notary, and participated in expeditions to conquer parts of neighboring Cuba. Cortés's efforts won favor with Hispaniola's governor, and he was appointed to a high political position in the colony.

Eventually, the governor asked Cortés to help him invade Mexico. The mainland was believed to hold a bonanza of silver and gold, and the governor put Cortés in command of an expedition to explore and secure the interior of the country for colonization.

Accompanied by around six hundred men, thirteen horses, and a small number of cannons, Cortés and his eleven ships landed on the Yucatán Peninsula. He claimed the land for the Spanish crown, won a few battles against the natives, and took over what is now Veracruz, a coastal region opposite the Gulf of Mexico from Cuba.

After he established a town, Cortés wanted to explore further. Tenochtitlán, two hundred miles inland, was supposed to be a magical city, full of infinite riches.

But at this point, Cortés and the governor were at odds. The governor feared losing control over the expedition and sent orders to relieve Cortés of his command. But Cortés went ahead anyway. Now he faced imprisonment or death if he returned to Cuba. His only option was to conquer and settle part of the land.

Not all Cortés's men were keen on pushing inland. Some were still loyal to the governor, and when they learned of their leader's plans, they conspired to seize a ship and sail back to Cuba.

Cortés moved quickly to quash their rebellion, but he faced a dilemma. For the mission to capture Tenochtitlán to succeed, he needed the men's allegiance. But with the ships readily available, it would be difficult to prevent another mutiny. If enough men snuck onto one of the boats, they could sail away and bring further repercussions from the governor.

Faced with this situation, Cortés made an unusual decision: to burn the ships. After removing the provisions and artillery from his ships, he ordered them put afire. All eleven of them.[12]

To prevent another mutiny, he had his own ships demolished.

Going back was no longer an option. Now everyone had to forge ahead.

What Cortés did might seem crazy. He didn't just make a statement; he destroyed his only option of getting home. But it turns out he wasn't the only person to adopt this strategy.

When invading the Iberian Peninsula in AD 711, Muslim commander Tariq ibn Ziyad ordered the burning of the ships he arrived in to prevent cowardice. An ancient Chinese saying, "Break the kettles and sink the boats," alludes to a battle in which a Chinese leader did something similar to encourage his army to commit to a course of action. And the expression "burning one's bridges" comes from the idea of burning a bridge after crossing it during a military campaign, leaving the troops no choice but to continue the march.

Compared to the situations most people face on a daily basis, this tactic is clearly extreme. And selfish.

But similar, less drastic versions can be applied to a broad set of situations in which people are stuck on the status quo. Not completely taking the old option off the table, but making people realize and bear more of its true costs.

Sam Michaels runs IT for a midsized entertainment firm. In addition to supporting the firm's website and other digital properties, Sam makes sure the company's software and hardware is running smoothly and is up to date.

Such updates should be relatively straightforward. Everyone installs the new version of Windows or gets an upgraded desktop when their old one becomes outdated. The new software has more features, and the new desktops are faster and more secure, so employees should be happy to upgrade.

But regardless of how great the upgrade is, Sam found that there were always some people who didn't want to switch. Rather than getting a new machine or new software, they preferred sticking with the old. Their existing machines were working fine, so they didn't want to take the time to learn a new operating system or risk files getting lost when they could stick with what they had.

Switching costs ruled the day.

And these laggards wouldn't budge. Sam could send

reminders, share links that showed how much better the upgrades would be, or even stop by their offices to plead in person, but they still weren't interested.

Eventually, Sam got tired of pushing, so he tried something else. He took the old option off the table.

One Monday morning Sam sent out an email to anyone who had yet to upgrade. In addition to recommending that people switch to a new machine, and providing some recommendations of how he could help them do so, Sam noted an upcoming change in IT support.

For security purposes, any machines that were still running Windows 7 in two months would have to be disconnected from the network. And because most employees had newer machines, and it was tough for IT to stay up to date on issues with older ones, at that point IT would no longer be able to support machines older than a certain vintage. If the machine broke down or had an issue, employees would have to address it themselves. IT preferred it didn't get that far and was happy to help employees get new machines, but if people didn't want to come along with the rest of the group, they were on their own.

Sam sent the email off and went out to lunch.

By the time he got back an hour later, half the people he emailed had responded asking to set up times when IT could help them with an upgrade. By the end of the week, the rest of the laggards had sent similar replies.

Sam's email worked because he burned the ships. He didn't go as far as Cortés. He didn't delete employees' old version of Windows or throw their computers out the window.

But he used the same principle. He surfaced the costs of

inaction and made it clear that soon those costs were going to increase. He made it clear that employees could still use the old ships, but if they wanted to do so, they would have to do it by themselves.

The same idea applies more broadly.

Car manufacturers don't refuse to make replacement parts for older vehicles, but once a reasonable time has passed, they stop making as many. Prices go up, and consumers are encouraged to transition to something new.

Manufacturers don't force consumers to change, but they also don't subsidize the prices on the old parts, leaving them artificially low. They pass the cost on to the consumer, making it less likely those consumers will stick with the status quo.

Inaction is easy. It requires little effort to stick with the same beliefs, little time to stick with the same policies and approaches, and little money to stick with products and services that are already being used.

Not surprisingly, then, when the choice is action or inaction, inaction often wins. Inertia prevails. A body at rest tends to stay at rest.

So sometimes inaction needs to be taken off the table. Or at least no longer subsidized. Because while inaction might beat newcomers in a royal rumble, once inaction becomes more costly, suddenly the contest is a lot more even. Now everyone is on equal footing.

Rather than thinking about *whether* a given new thing is better than the old one, by helping to take inaction off the table, burning the ships encourages people to set aside the old and instead think about *which* new thing is worth pursuing.

Easing Endowment

Returning to the mug study: people are attached to things they're already doing. Whether it's the products they own or beliefs they hold, the suppliers they work with or the initiatives they support.

Catalyzing change isn't just about making people more comfortable with *new* things; it's about helping them let go of *old* ones. Easing endowment. Like financial advisor Gloria Barrett, we need to surface the cost of inaction, helping people realize that inaction and the status quo aren't as costless as they seem. Like Sam Michaels in IT, we need to burn the ships, taking the status quo off the table, or at least stop subsidizing its cost.

And to see the power of easing endowment in action, we need look no further than one of the biggest election upsets in recent history: the referendum on Brexit.

How to Change a Nation's Opinion

On May 21, 2015, Dominic Cummings agreed to help start an organization that would eventually be called Vote Leave. The next day he began the monumental task of getting Britons to give up their almost fifty-year membership in the European Union.

Unlike traditional policy making, referendums are determined by public opinion. Rather than a small set of politicians deciding whether the UK should stay in the EU, the minimum wage should be increased, or any number of other questions, these ballot measures invite the entire electorate to cast their vote.

Most referendums fail. In Oregon and California, for example, the two states with the highest number of statewide initiatives on the ballot, only about a third of referendums pass. Worldwide, the number is only slightly larger.

For referendums to succeed, millions of people have to be persuaded to change. To raise the minimum wage from what it is to something higher. To abandon forty-six years of economic integration, agricultural subsidies, and free trade. To give up the old way of doing things and switch to something new.

In the UK's case, the risk of leaving the EU was particularly profound. Most of the UK's food, fuel, and medicine is imported, so any slowdown in trade could generate shortages. Economists were worried about the impact on exports and concerned that a departure would devalue the British pound.

Not surprisingly, then, few thought the referendum would pass. Most polls suggested that the UK would stay in the EU. Bookmakers had the same outlook, with the betting odds implying an 80 percent probability of victory for the pro-EU camp.

Cummings recognized that referendums face a messaging challenge. The status quo is fundamentally easier to explain. It doesn't require unpacking why the EU is bad for Brits or how the complex flow of subsidies, grants, and other support might or might not balance out the money the UK was investing in the European Union. All the "Remain" campaign had to do was tell people to stay the course. Do what they had always done. Just don't mess things up.

If the "Leave" side had even a chance of staging an upset, they couldn't get stuck in the weeds. They needed a simple message that anyone could understand.

So Cummings bought a big red bus for Vote Leave. He had politicians drive around the country, speaking to voters. And on the side of the bus in large white letters it read: "We send the EU £350 million a week; let's fund our NHS [National Health Service] instead."[13]

The Brexit bus, as it came to be called, didn't just grab attention; it surfaced the costs of inaction. Brits might think that staying in the EU was safer. That it was costless. But the bus showed them otherwise. That each week the UK was sending hundreds of millions of pounds in membership fees to the EU. Money that could be spent on things like the National Health Service instead.

But the bus also did something else. Because below that message, in slightly smaller font, Cummings placed the rallying cry for the entire Leave campaign.

The slogan started as just two words: "Take control." Cummings loved its simplicity but felt something was missing. So he played around with different variations.

Cummings was well versed in loss aversion and the status quo bias. He knew that people prefer to stick with things they're already doing rather than do something new. And while "Take control" was fine, it implicitly agreed to the premise that leaving the EU was action and staying was inaction. Which played right into his opponents' hands.

If only he could flip things around . . . make it seem like *leaving* was the status quo . . .

So, in a stroke of insight, he changed the slogan. It wasn't much: just an extra word in between "Take" and "control." But it completely changed the reference point.

He added the word "back." As in "Take back control."

"'Back,'" Cummings wrote in his blog, "plays into a strong evolved instinct—we hate losing things, especially control." "Back" triggered loss aversion. It made it seem like something had been lost, and that leaving the EU was a way to regain that.

When the British Election Study surveyed voters, four times as many people preferred the "Let's take back control" language. And when votes were tallied on June 23, there was a shocking result. Britons voted to leave the European Union.

With "Let's take back control," Cummings cleverly reframed the entire debate. He took the endowment effect, and people's increased valuation for what they have, and reminded them that the UK used to be outside the EU. Leaving wasn't risky; it was simply a way of righting the ship.* Returning things to how they were.

This strategy isn't always easy to apply. It may not be immediately obvious how a new drug or manufacturing process can be framed as helping to regain a loss.

But in many cases this approach is a cunning way to turn the tables on inertia. Even though he wasn't the incumbent, Donald Trump famously used this idea in his 2016 presidential run. Rather than saying he would make America great, he said he would make America great *again*. That he would help return things to where they were. Ronald Reagan used similar messaging in his 1980 presidential campaign.

And it's not just politics. School districts talk about how their curriculums are "back to basics." Organizations talk about how a new approach or focus helps them return to their roots. Rather than highlighting how ideas, policies, or initiatives are new, they focus on how similar they are to things that came before.

Even new products and services can be talked about this way. It's the same thing you've always known and loved, just updated for today's digital age.

It's not a change; it's a refresh.

---

* It was also about taking back control of the system itself. It made people think. "Yeah, these are the guys who screwed up the economy, who drove it off a cliff in 2008, whose mates are all Goldman Sachs bankers with hedge funds on massive bonuses," said Cummings. "We'll take back control from you lot in London."

Reactance and endowment are two important barriers that prevent change. But to understand why information often fails to shift people's position, we have to appreciate the importance of distance.

3. Distance

When Virginia[1] knocked, it was always hard to know how people would react. Young, wearing a white T-shirt and glasses, Virginia looked friendly enough that most people would at least open the door to find out what was going on.

Today, as part of a group of political canvassers, Virginia was asking Miami voters how they felt about transgender rights. The Miami–Dade County Commission had recently passed an ordinance protecting transgender people from discrimination, and it was a contentious topic with strong opinions on both sides.

"What number feels right for you?" Virginia asked Gustavo, pointing to a scale on a sheet of paper, with numbers spanning from strongly against transgender rights to strongly for them.

Standing in his doorway in a sleeveless undershirt tucked into khaki pants, the older Latino man looked as traditional as they come. Add a guayabera shirt, and Gustavo could have been a member of the Buena Vista Social Club. Virginia, on the other hand, is a gender-nonconforming person who identifies as neither male nor female.

Gustavo pointed to a number on the bottom half of the scale, indicating he opposed the legislation. "And you feel that way because of the bathroom situation?" Virginia asked. Gustavo said he wouldn't support the legislation because he's worried how it might be used. How predatory men could take it as an opportunity to enter women's bathrooms.

"Where does that come from, that feeling?" Virginia inquired.

"Because I'm from South America," Gustavo said, "and in South America we don't like fags."

Hearing that was like a slap in the face. Most people would politely thank the voter for their time and walk away. Most people would say that it's not worth it to try to sway—that it's not *possible* to sway—someone like Gustavo, who has such a viscerally held, viscerally worded belief.

But could that intuition be wrong? Might there be a way to change someone like Gustavo's mind? Can even committed conservatives be convinced to support "liberal" policies like transgender rights?

Reaching Across the Aisle

To say the current political climate in the United States is divisive is an understatement. More than half of Democrats and Republicans have "very unfavorable" feelings toward the opposing party, more than three times the number in the mid-1990s. Neighbors tear down yard signs, opposing perspectives are shunned, and many a Thanksgiving dinner is served with reminders not to discuss politics.

So-called filter bubbles are a common explanation for the discord. Birds of a feather have always flocked together, and people have always preferred media outlets that support their existing views, but technology has exacerbated these tendencies.

Rather than talking to neighbors or paging through local papers, people get their news and information online. And the online eco-system is increasingly tailored to one's existing views. Facebook prioritizes information from your closest contacts, who often share similar perspectives. Twitter only shows you information from the people you follow, who often already agree with you.

The Web and social media have combined to create a state of intellectual isolationism where people are rarely exposed to conflicting viewpoints. Combined with people's penchant for clicking on information that supports their perspectives, these algorithms can lead humanity to become more and more isolated in their own echo chambers.

To solve this problem, pundits suggest reaching across the aisle. Rather than holing up inside one's online bubble, talking to someone who sees things differently. Create bridges to the other side.

Intuitively, this makes a lot of sense. By moving beyond caricatures and stereotypes and engaging with someone who disagrees, both sides will benefit. Rather than snowflakes or deplorables, people will start to see the other side as real human beings. By understanding where the opposition is coming from, we'll all gain more nuanced views.

But does that actually work?

Sociologist Chris Bail was hopeful.[2] He thought if you could just get people to consider the other side, they'd come around. That exposure to opposing viewpoints would shift people to-ward the middle. Not a lot, but some. Liberals and conservatives wouldn't be singing "Kumbaya," but they'd at least move slightly toward the other party.

To test this possibility, Bail set up a clever experiment. He recruited more than 1,500 Twitter users and had them follow accounts that exposed them to opposing viewpoints. For a month they saw messages and information from elected officials, organizations, and opinion leaders from the other side. A liberal might see tweets from Fox News or Donald Trump. A conservative might see posts from Hillary Clinton or Planned Parenthood.

It was a digital version of reaching across the aisle. A simple intervention that could have big effects for social policy.

Then, at the end of the month, Bail and his team measured users' attitudes. How they felt about various political and social issues. Things like whether government regulation is beneficial, whether homosexuality should be accepted by society, and whether the best way to ensure peace is through military strength.

It was a huge undertaking. Years of preparation and thousands of hours of work. The hope was that, as thousands of pundits, columnists, and other talking heads have argued, connecting with the other side would bring people closer together.

But that's not what happened. Exposure to the other side didn't make people more moderate.

In fact, just the opposite. Exposure to opposing views *did* change minds, but in the opposite direction. Rather than becoming more liberal, Republicans exposed to liberal information became more conservative, developing more extreme attitudes toward social policies. Liberals showed similar effects. Democrats who followed a conservative account became *more* liberal, not less.

It would be one thing if the tweets had tried to persuade. As discussed in the first chapter, persuasive attempts often induce reactance.

But in this instance, rather than telling people to do something, most posts just contained information.

So why didn't information help?

Correcting False Beliefs

When trying to change minds, we hope that evidence will work. That giving people facts, figures, and other information will encourage them to move in our direction.

The intuition is simple. Data should lead people to update their thinking. They should consider the evidence provided and shift their opinions accordingly.

Unfortunately, that doesn't always happen.

Take false information. Vaccines help protect people against diseases like the measles, mumps, and rubella (MMR). But even though most people get vaccinated, some parents fail to immunize their kids due to unfounded concerns about links between vaccines and autism.

In a 2014 article in the journal *Pediatrics*, researchers examined whether exposing people to the truth could help change false beliefs.[3] They presented people with scientific evidence from the Centers for Disease Control that debunked the vaccine/autism link. It noted that "many carefully performed scientific studies have found no link between MMR vaccine and autism," and summarized some of the different findings from different studies.

After reading the article, participants provided their own opinions. How likely would they be to give a future child the MMR vaccine?

Did exposure to the truth help? Sort of.

For people who were already favorably disposed toward

vaccines, the additional information helped. It reduced misperceptions and increased their intent to vaccinate their kids.

But for participants with less favorable attitudes toward vaccines, exposure to the truth backfired. Providing scientific evidence from the CDC didn't correct the misinformation. In fact, just the opposite: it made them *less* likely to want to vaccinate their kids.

Numerous studies have found similar effects.[4] Whether examining medicine, politics, or other areas, evidence that was supposed to change minds didn't always work. Sometimes it made people more likely to believe the truth, but other times it just reaffirmed falsehoods. Even though there was little intent to persuade—so presumably little reactance—people still discounted the information.

Rather than changing false beliefs, exposure to the truth often *increased* misperceptions. Giving people correct information made them more likely to believe the exact opposite.

So when does information work and when does it backfire?

A Football Field of Beliefs

Over a half century ago, behavioral scientists from Yale, Vanderbilt, and the University of Oklahoma tried to answer this question.[5] It was the late 1950s and they wanted to pick a controversial issue. Something where different people would have different opinions and where it would be easy to compare messages advocating various positions.

They chose booze.

While most of the United States had repealed prohibition decades before, the sale of alcohol was still prohibited in Oklahoma, where the experiment was conducted. The state had recently held a referendum to determine the fate of the existing laws, and the vote favored prohibition by a narrow margin. Some Oklahomans were against prohibition, but slightly more were for maintaining the alcohol restriction. It was the perfect issue to investigate.

The experimenters created different written appeals. One was very anti-prohibition. It noted that many people like drinking, so the sale and use of alcohol should not be restricted.

The second appeal took a more moderate anti-prohibition tone. It suggested things like "the sale of alcohol should be regulated so that it is available in limited quantities for special occasions."

Then, they recruited prohibition supporters (e.g., members of the Women's Christian Temperance Union and students preparing to become priests and nuns), gave them one of the two anti-prohibition messages, and measured attitude change. How much respondents' views toward alcohol shifted as a result of being exposed to the message.

One might imagine that taking a more extreme stance would generate more change. After all, in everything from salary negotiations to buying a home, people usually start by asking for more rather than less.

Home buyers offer 85 to 90 percent of the asking price initially with the hope of meeting somewhere in the middle, so sellers list things artificially high to start. By asking for more, sellers make sure to reach their desired outcome even after haggling is taken into account.

Applied to changing minds, staking out a farther position takes advantage of this tendency to split the difference. Even if people don't move all the way, meeting in the middle means ending up closer to the desired endpoint. Meeting the strongly worded anti-prohibition appeal halfway would mean a greater change than meeting the moderately worded appeal halfway.

But that's not what happened. When researchers analyzed the results of the prohibition study, they found that the strong appeal wasn't more effective in changing minds.

And the reason why is something called the region of rejection.

Before giving respondents one of the two anti-prohibition appeals, researchers solicited their current opinions toward alcohol and prohibition. Participants were shown eight statements and circled the one that came closest to their point of view. Some statements strongly supported prohibition, some strongly opposed it, and others fell somewhere in between.

Imagine a football field divided by hash marks, with different marks indicating different prohibition views. One side supports prohibition, the other side opposes it, and the two end zones are the people who feel most strongly.

The supporters' end zone is filled with people who strongly support prohibition. They most agree with statements like "Since alcohol is the curse of mankind, the sale and use of alcohol, including light beer, should be completely abolished."

The opposition end zone wants to completely repeal prohibition. They agree most with statements like "It has become evident that man cannot get along without alcohol; therefore, there should be no restriction whatsoever on its sale and use."

Move toward midfield, however, and the extremism tempers. Around the 25-yard lines are people who are mildly for or against prohibition. They are fine keeping some restrictions on alcohol but feel like it should be available in small quantities for reasonable occasions. And on the 50-yard line are people on the fence. They feel that the arguments in favor and against are nearly equal.

In addition to picking the statement that best represented their opinion, respondents also noted which views they didn't find objectionable and which ones they disagreed with or couldn't see supporting.

These choices created two zones. One was the *zone of acceptance*. The perspective that people agreed with the most, along with the range of viewpoints they could see potentially supporting.

Beyond this safe area was the *region of rejection*. The range of perspectives people strongly disagreed with or actively rejected as wrong.

Take someone whose views put them at midfield. That's their current opinion, but their zone of acceptance would be any positions in either direction that they might support. Beyond that is the region of rejection, or anything they would not consider.

Different people not only have different positions on the field, their zones of acceptance and regions of rejection vary as well. One person might be in one end zone with a zone of acceptance up to the 20-yard line and a region of rejection for anything beyond that.

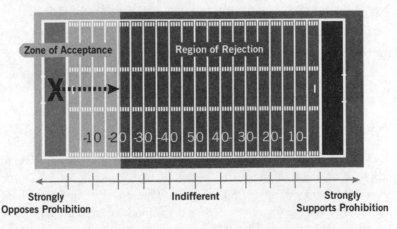

Another might be on the 25-yard line, accepting anything on that half while rejecting everything on the other side.

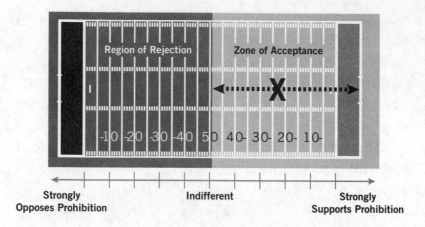

These different zones, in turn, determined whether the anti-prohibition messages succeeded or failed. Incoming information was compared with people's existing views. If the content was close enough (i.e., within their zone of acceptance), the information worked as intended. People changed their mind in the desired direction.

But if the information fell in the region of rejection, it failed. Not only did the content not persuade, it often backfired. People changed their minds in the *opposite* direction. They became even more certain their initial views were right.*

---

* The same holds in politics. Republicans don't only listen to conservative news and Democrats don't only follow liberal media. Depending on where people sit on the continuum, they're willing to consider or listen to some perspectives and not others. An extremely liberal Democrat might think *Slate* is even-handed but not even consider something from the *Wall Street Journal*, while a more moderate Democrat might think Slate is extreme and consider more conservative views all the way up to Fox News.

Overall, the moderate appeal led almost three times as many prohibition supporters to move toward legalizing alcohol.[6]

Sometimes less is better than more.

The Confirmation Bias

When trying to change minds, we often want big change right away. We want a big raise now. We want detractors to immediately become supporters.

We think that if we just give people enough information, they'll come around. If we just share more evidence, list more reasons, or put together the right deck, people will switch.

But just as often this blows up in our faces. Rather than shifting perspectives, people dig in their heels. Rather than changing, they become even more convinced they're right.

As we discussed, reactance is one reason. When people feel like someone is trying to convince them, their guard goes up. They counterargue against the persuasion.

But even when there is no attempt to persuade, sometimes even just providing information backfires.

And the region of rejection explains why. People have a range, or zone around their beliefs that they are willing to consider. Staunch conservatives oppose government spending and regulation. Tell them about a bill to eliminate deficit spending or protect free markets, and they'll probably support it.

But go beyond that zone, to things like raising the debt ceiling or providing universal health care, and it backfires. The further afield the message, the less likely they'll listen. And the more likely it will push them in the opposite direction.

Because the region of rejection not only impacts change, it

shapes how people perceive and react to information. People search for, interpret, and favor information in a way that confirms or supports their existing beliefs.

After watching a football game between Princeton and Dartmouth, for example, students from each university were asked several follow-up questions.[7] It was a rough game, and many penalties were called on both teams. Dartmouth's quarterback had his leg broken after being tackled in the backfield. Princeton's star tailback got a broken nose and mild concussion. Princeton ended up winning, but tempers flared on both sides and there were heated discussions about who was at fault.

How fans saw the game, though, depended entirely on which side they supported. Princeton students thought Dartmouth started the rough play and committed twice as many penalties as their own side. Dartmouth students thought both sides had been rough and that Princeton had caused more penalties. Exact same game, two very different perspectives.[8]

These biases even shape whether people believe seemingly objective things like scientific research.

Professors at Stanford University gave people information about two studies that examined the efficacy of the death penalty.[9] One study, whose findings suggested the death penalty worked as a deterrent, compared murder rates the year before and after the adoption of capital punishment in fourteen states. It found that in eleven of the fourteen states, murder rates were lower after adoption of the death penalty.

The other study, whose findings suggested the death penalty was not a deterrent, compared murder rates in ten pairs of neighboring states with different capital punishment laws. It found that in eight of the ten pairs, murder rates were *higher* in the state with capital punishment.

In addition to the study results, participants were given information about how the research was conducted: procedural details about the methods and so on.

Then participants were asked how convincing they found the study and about the quality of the research, i.e., whether each study was well done or poorly conducted.

While it makes sense that team loyalties might affect how a game is seen, one would hope responses to scientific research would be more objective—particularly in such an important domain like the death penalty, where lives are on the line.

But it turned out that how people perceived these seemingly objective scientific results depended entirely on their position on the field. People who supported the death penalty thought the study suggesting it was an effective deterrent was more convincing. Death penalty opponents thought the exact opposite.

The same held for how well they thought the studies had been done. People who supported the death penalty thought the study suggesting it was an effective deterrent was "well thought out" and "seemed to have gathered data properly." Opponents argued that "the evidence given is relatively meaningless without data about how the overall crime rate went up in those years." For the study that found the death penalty ineffective, the perspectives were reversed. While death penalty opponents said things like "Using neighboring states helps to make the experiment more accurate [because they are] similar locations," supporters said things like "There might be very different circumstances between the sets of two states, even though they were sharing a border."

Even seemingly objective "facts" hinged on the preexisting

beliefs of the people interpreting those facts. People's decision to accept the findings or search for flaws depended less on the specific procedures employed and more on whether its results aligned with their existing beliefs.

No wonder one person's truth is another's "fake news." Whether information seems true or false depends on one's position on the field. Rather than uniting opposing sides, exposure to evidence sometimes just widens the gap.

This tendency to look for and process information in a way that confirms one's existing viewpoint has been called the confirmation bias.[10] And no one is immune. Confirmation bias shapes the treatments doctors prescribe, decisions jurors make, and strategies investors follow. It drives what actions leaders take, research scientists pursue, and feedback employees internalize.

As psychologist Thomas Gilovich noted, "When examining evidence relevant to a given belief, people are inclined to see what they expect to see, and conclude what they expect to conclude . . . For desired conclusions . . . we ask ourselves, '*Can* I believe this?,' but for unpalatable conclusions we ask, '*Must* I believe this?' "*

---

* This bias even extends to extremists, such as members of Stormfront .org, the largest white pride online discussion forum. The forum defines being white as "non-Jewish people of wholly European descent. No exceptions," and members of the site often take genetic tests to prove their whiteness. But what happens when those test results show that they fail to meet their own criteria? Researchers found that many members whose test results suggested they weren't of wholly European descent came up with

These biases make changing minds all the more difficult. Not only do people have to be willing to change, they have to be willing to listen to information that might open them up to that possibility.

When ideas or information comes in, people compare it to their existing view. They consider and weigh it to understand how it fits with existing beliefs.

If it falls within the zone of acceptance, it gets the seal of approval. It's marked as trustworthy, safe, and dependable. And it shifts people in that direction.

But if the ideas or information falls in the region of rejection, it faces deeper scrutiny. It's seen as unreliable, anecdotal, and erroneous, or, even worse, ignored completely.[11] And shifts attitudes in the opposite direction.*

So how can we combat these biases? How do catalysts avoid the region of rejection and encourage people to actually consider what they have to say?

Three ways to mitigate distance are to (1) find the movable middle, (2) ask for less, and (3) switch the field to find an unsticking point.

---

an excuse. The test results must be biased, or genetic tests aren't really the right way to measure "whiteness" anyway. Even white nationalists change their standards when those standards don't fit what they want them to.

* The converse also holds. Whether people see information as true or false shapes which side they attribute it to. If people think information is true, they think it came from their side. If they think it's false, it must have come from the opposition.

Find the Movable Middle

Every election cycle, political campaigns lay out huge sums of money. In 2016, for example, more than $6.5 billion was spent on the presidential and congressional elections.

Although some money is spent on staff, food, and transportation, most of it is spent on persuasion. Direct mail, phone banking, and door-to-door canvassing. Television, radio, and digital ads that try to convince people to vote one way or the other.

There is some evidence that this money is well spent. When political scientists looked across dozens of studies of primaries and ballot measures, they found a clear pattern.[12] Advertising and campaign contact worked. Things like direct mail and door-to-door canvassing influenced how voters evaluated the candidates and shifted who they voted for.

But when they analyzed general elections, the political scientists found something different. One would expect the same results. After all, just like primaries, races to decide who will be president or hold a given Senate seat still involve contacting voters and running ads to convince people to do one thing or another.

However, across dozens of studies, the political scientists found that the average effect of things like direct mail and canvassing on general elections was . . . zero. And while it was harder to evaluate the effectiveness of digital and television advertising, the evidence they found was similarly damning. Zero effect.

Just to be sure, they conducted a few more tests. They ran new experiments, studying thousands of respondents. But while this approach increased statistical precision tenfold, it still netted the same result. No effect.

Why?

Well, the answer lies with the difference between primaries and general elections. Both involve multiple candidates competing against one another, laying out their stands on different issues, and trying to win over voters.

But rather than running against members of their own party, as in primaries, general elections usually involve running against someone from the opposing party. While primaries involve deciding between two candidates who've staked out positions on the same side of the field, general elections involve candidates who sit on completely different halves. Not only may the two options be further apart, one is likely within the zone of acceptance, while the other is likely in the region of rejection.

Consequently, changing minds becomes a lot harder. It's one thing to get Democrats to support a Democratic candidate who is slightly more liberal than they are, but getting them to support a Republican is a lot more challenging.

This is particularly true given the strength of party affiliations. Feeling strongly about an issue or domain changes the breadth of information people are willing to consider. People who don't care about a given domain or issue have a wide zone of acceptance and a small region of rejection. There are many positions they would be amenable to and few they would reject outright.

But for people who care a lot, it's the exact opposite. They see things as right and wrong, meaning there is only a narrow range of perspectives they would consider. A small zone of acceptance and a wide region of rejection.[13]

This is part of why changing political views is so challenging. You're not just trying to change positions slightly; you're trying to get people to switch sides. And not just on any issue. One they feel strongly about and about which they are unlikely to listen to

alternate perspectives. It's like asking a Red Sox fan to start root-
ing for the Yankees, or asking a Coke drinker to switch to Pepsi.
Not the easiest ask.

So what's one to do in situations like these? Just give up?

Not quite. Because the election study found a silver lining.
One place where candidates changed minds in general elections
even when change seemed difficult.

And that was by finding the movable middle.

In politics, smart campaigns don't try to change *every* mind;
they focus on swing voters who are open to facts and arguments.
Undecideds, or pockets of people who, given the candidate, cir-
cumstance, or issue, are receptive to being swayed. People who
have a larger zone of acceptance or whose zone overlaps more
with the candidate's positions.

And rather than using the same arguments on everyone, catalysts use a more surgical approach. They target people with specific messages that are most relevant to them.

In Oregon in 2008, for example, Democrat Jeff Merkley was
running against incumbent Republican Gordon Smith for U.S.
Senate. Smith was a popular politician and generally viewed as a
moderate, so the race was gearing up to be quite competitive.

Researchers were interested to see whether they could change
voters' minds.[14] Whether they could shift people who would
have voted for the incumbent Republican to vote for the Democratic challenger.

But instead of carpet-bombing everyone with the same appeal,
they worked to find people who might already be predisposed.
Voters who, for whatever reason, might be more willing to
change their minds.

First, they looked for a wedge. An issue where the incumbent was out of step with at least some of his constituents.

After sifting through various possibilities, they landed on abortion. Oregonians tend to be pro-choice, and the incumbent Republican senator was not. Even better, the challenger was one of a handful of Senate candidates that the National Association for the Repeal of Abortion Laws, or NARAL Pro-Choice America, was endorsing that year.

Then the researchers identified pro-choice voters and tried to persuade them based on that specific issue. Earlier in that election cycle, advocacy groups had conducted a large-scale survey identifying voters who supported women's right to choose. Through both phone calls and mailings, the researchers targeted this group, highlighting Merkley's endorsement by Planned Parenthood and NARAL Pro-Choice America and his opponent's repeated pro-life votes in the Senate.

Would that approach work on all voters? Definitely not. The economy dominated the election, and abortion was not the most important thing for everyone.

Further, sending everyone the same message could have easily backfired. For folks who don't care about abortion, it would have fallen on deaf ears, and for pro-life advocates it probably would have boomeranged and increased support for the incumbent.

But by going after the movable middle, this campaign shifted voting by almost 10 percent. And the challenger Merkley won.

When dealing with issues that people feel strongly about, start by finding the movable middle. Individuals who, by virtue of their existing positions, are more likely to shift because they're not so far away to begin with.

One way is to look for behavioral residue. Clues that indicate conflicting opinions or a willingness to change. In the political context, Blue Dog Democrats who support gun rights or Republicans who've signed a petition supporting environmental reform. In a business context, consumers who've complained about a competitor on social media.

High-tech approaches such as lookalike targeting can also be useful. Leveraging data on existing customers or supporters to find others who have similar characteristics and preferences and thus are more likely to be interested.

And when data isn't already available, test and learn. Take a sample of people, test a particular approach, and record key characteristics on various dimensions. Using that to identify subgroups or pockets where the approach was particularly effective can help determine what types of people to go after in the population more broadly.

Trying to get a new product to take off? Rather than trying to convince everyone how great it is, find the subgroup that already needs it. Venture capitalists often refer to products and services as vitamins or painkillers. Nice-to-haves (e.g., vitamins) that can be put off until later, or need-to-haves (e.g., painkillers) that people can't live without.

Rather than going after anyone, catalysts start by finding the people who see their offering as a painkiller. Locating potential users who need the offering and can't wait to sign up.

Trying to change minds in a meeting? Start with the people whose position is closest to begin with. Not only are they more likely to come around, but by changing their minds, they'll hopefully become advocates and bring others along with them.

Ask for Less

The movable middle is a great place to start, but sometimes we want to change minds of people who are further away. So how do we do that?

Imagine sitting at work, when you get a call on your cell phone. The caller introduces themselves as a representative from the Consumers' Group and asks if you'd be willing to participate in a survey. It will involve them coming to your home to categorize all your household products. And to make sure they get all the necessary information, they'll need to have full access to your entire home. Including all your cupboards and storage spaces, just in case they need to root through them. Five, maybe six people will come by and it shouldn't take more than a couple hours. And they're asking if you'll do all this on a volunteer basis. In other words, for free.

Willing to participate?

If you're trying to stifle laughter at the audacity of this request, you wouldn't be alone. Five or six people coming by my house to root through the cupboards? No way! Who would be crazy enough to even ask for such a thing? And volunteer to do it for free? Not a chance.

A request like this clearly falls in the region of rejection. It's just too much to endure.

Indeed, when two Stanford psychologists called people up and made a similar request, barely more than a handful said yes.[15] We're not sure who these kind souls were or whether they even understood what they agreed to. Most people, not surprisingly, said no.

The psychologists were interested in a problem everyone faces daily. How to get people to do something they'd rather not do.

And as the scientists noted, the most common way of attacking this problem is through pushing: "Exert as much pressure as possible on the reluctant individual . . . to force him to comply." Tell them they should do it. Punish them if they don't do it. Pay them so that they will do it. Push, push, push until they give in.

The scientists thought there might be a better approach.

And there was. When the researchers asked a different group of people, more than twice as many said yes.

Same ask. Same volunteering for a half dozen people to tramp through your home for two hours. But this time, more than half the people agreed.

The difference?

The scientists started by asking for less.

Three days earlier they had called the second group of people with a much more innocuous request. They gave respondents the same story (that they were calling from the Consumers' Group), but rather than starting with the big request (riffling through their cupboards), the scientists started with a smaller one instead. Whether respondents would be willing to answer a few questions over the phone about what household products they owned. Simple things like what brand of soap they used to clean the dishes.

Most people who picked up the phone were happy to help. Sure, answering a few questions wasn't their favorite thing to do, but it wasn't in the region of rejection, either.

And when the scientists called back a couple days later with the much larger request? These people were much more likely to agree.

The researchers found that completing that first, small request changed how people saw themselves. Initially, answering a couple of questions over the phone might have been the most that someone was willing to do; it was at the edge of their zone of acceptance. But agreeing to that ask shifted their position. It changed where they stood on the field. As the scientists noted: "Once he has agreed to a request . . . he may become, in his own eyes, the kind of person who does this sort of thing."

Agreeing to a small, related ask moved people in the right direction. Which meant that the final ask, which once would have been too far away, was now within the zone of acceptance.

Because when people move their position on the field, their zones and regions move with them. Consequently, rather than being squarely in the region of rejection, the final ask is now in more people's zone of acceptance. Which makes them more likely to help.

Having a tough time changing someone's mind? Try asking for less rather than pushing for more. Dial down the size of the initial request so that it falls within the zone of acceptance. Not only will that make that initial request more successful, it also makes big change more likely overall.

Doctors often deal with this when trying to help obese people cut weight. When someone needs to lose 50 or 100 pounds, the tendency is to ask for something drastic. Exercise every day. Stop eating junk food. Completely cut out dessert.

But these approaches inevitably fail. Such recommendations are great in theory, but people are unlikely to listen, and they're hard to implement. Sure, an obese person *should* exercise once a day, but for someone who hasn't worked out in months or years, that's a big ask.

Dr. Diane Priest was trying to help an obese truck driver lose weight. The guy liked Mountain Dew, and liter bottles were easy to take on the road with him, so he was drinking up to three a day.

Three liters of Mountain Dew? That's over 60 grams of sugar. And doing it every day? That's like eating over one hundred Snickers bars a month.

The best thing would be for the truck driver to stop drinking soda entirely. But Dr. Priest knew that would be a tough sell. So she started with a smaller ask.

Try drinking just two liters a day, she said. Two bottles rather than three. And every time you use the restroom, fill up an old liter bottle with water so that you have that instead.

It was difficult at first, but the truck driver eventually went from three liters of Mountain Dew a day, to two.

Then Dr. Priest asked him to cut it down to one. And once that worked, only then did she suggest cutting out soda entirely.

The trucker driver still drinks a can of Mountain Dew now and then, but he's lost over 25 pounds.[16]

When trying to change minds, the tendency is to go big. We want to shift people's perspective right away. We're looking for that silver bullet pitch that will immediately get someone to quit drinking soda or switch political parties overnight.

But look closer at big changes, and they're rarely that abrupt. Instead, they're often more of a process. A slow and steady shift with many stages along the way.

Asking for less is about committing to that process. Dr. Priest started by asking the truck driver to drink one fewer bottle of

Mountain Dew, but she didn't stop there. She asked for less initially and then asked for a little more.

Rather than just asking for less, then, it's really about *chunking the change*. Breaking big asks into smaller, more manageable chunks. Starting with one and building from there. Moving 10 or 15 yards at a time, rather than tossing a Hail Mary and hoping for the best.

Product designers talk about this as building stepping-stones. If Uber's initial offering involved asking users to get into a stranger's car, the company probably would never have gotten off the ground. Accept a ride from strangers? That's exactly what Mom told you not to do.

Instead, the company started with a much smaller ask. They launched as an easier way to hail executive car service. With the motto "Everyone's private driver," people could order up exclusive rides in black luxury cars. Only after that initial high-end positioning succeeded did they move down-market to UberX, a cheaper option that offered non-luxury vehicles (but still subject to a background check). Eventually they hope to move to entirely autonomous vehicles.

If Uber had asked people to make such a big change initially, they probably would have failed. It was too far from what people were used to. Too different from what most consumers felt safe doing. But by chunking the change, they shrank the size of the ask. Each new product launch was like a stepping-stone, slowly moving consumers from what they were used to toward something new and different.

Ask someone to wade across a raging river and they'll probably say no. It's scary. The water's too deep. I might get swept away by the current.

But add stepping-stones along the way, and people will be much more willing to take the journey. Now they can hop from one side to the other without worrying about getting wet.*

Switch the Field; Find an Unsticking Point

Asking for less shrinks the distance. It provides a stepping-stone. And in so doing, it makes that final ask ever closer and ever more reachable.

But when someone is really dug in, there is one more technique that is often useful. And that is to switch the field. Find a dimension where there's already agreement and use that as a pivot point.

What would it take to help people to become less prejudiced?

Dave Fleischer has been asking himself that question since he was six years old. He grew up in the only Jewish family in Chillicothe, Ohio, and to make matters even more complicated, he was

---

* One place to start is to highlight ways people already agree or are already moving on in the desired direction. One diet and exercise book cleverly leverages this idea. Rather than starting off by trying to convince people to be healthier, the author points out that this is something they already want: "Congratulations! Whether you realize it or not, simply by picking up this book you have taken the first of what I hope will be many steps, both large and small, simple and challenging, toward the most rewarding journey of all—the road to reclaiming your physical health, well-being, and happiness." By pointing out ways people are already on board, the author encourages readers to see their position on the field as closer to the end goal. Which makes them likely to stick around for the next phase of the journey (Greene, 2002, p. 9).[17]

gay. "If I would have only talked to people who agreed with me, I would have only talked to my mom and dad," he said.

Now in his sixties, Dave has spent a lifetime trying to reduce prejudice. His firsthand experience as an outsider led him to community organizing, and he's helped get out the vote for various political causes.

In November 2008, though, Fleischer got a wake-up call. California residents were voting on Proposition 8, a measure that proposed banning same-sex marriage in the state. Given California's liberal leanings, the polls suggested the measure would be soundly defeated and the pro-LGBT side would win.

But they didn't. The measure passed.

It was a huge blow to the community. People were shocked and outraged. They didn't know what to make of the situation or what to do next.

As Dave tried to make sense of the loss, he had an idea. Rather than make assumptions about the people who voted against them, why not ask them directly? Go to the neighborhoods where they had been crushed, seek out the voters who had voted against them, and ask them why they did that.

Working with the Los Angeles LGBT Center, Dave and his team went to the heart of the counties where they lost. Places where people were staunchly opposed to gay marriage or hated gays and lesbians. Canvassers knocked on doors and talked to Prop 8 supporters to understand their perspectives.

Canvassing usually follows a carefully designed script. A political consultant architects a message, and the canvassers' job is to deliver the pitch. Word for word, spewing facts and figures to try to convince people to go along. The conversations, if you can call them that, are usually one-sided and often feel forced. Like being lectured to. Not surprisingly, many voters rush to end the interaction.

In the aftermath of Proposition 8, though, Dave's team tried to stop talking and start listening. No script, just asking people why they felt the way they did.

Over 15,000 one-on-one conversations later, Fleischer and his team learned far more than they expected. Not just about people's preferences regarding gay marriage, but about what it took to change voters' hearts and minds. They went through seventy-four different iterations of the script before they finally settled on one they liked. They called the new approach "deep canvassing."

Few things are more resistant to change than prejudice. More than fifty years after the Civil Rights Act outlawed discrimination based on race, sex, or national origin, intolerance is still alive and well. Over half of Americans express anti-black prejudice and a third are against gay marriage. In just the past few years a Yale University student called the police when she found an African American student napping in the dorm common room, and U.S. Customs and Border Protection agents detained two women just for speaking Spanish at a Montana gas station.

Part of the challenge is how deeply ingrained prejudice often is. Kids acquire beliefs from their parents, religion, or other social ties, and these perspectives become part of their worldview, almost second nature.

Not surprisingly, then, when Dave showed videos of his deep canvassing approach to a prominent political scientist, the professor was skeptical that it actually changed anyone's mind. "There's no reason to think you're succeeding," he said, "because nobody has."

To provide a more rigorous test, in June 2015, Fleischer helped conduct an experiment in Florida.[18] A few months earlier, Miami–Dade County had passed an ordinance protecting transgender people from discrimination. Fearing a backlash, volunteers and staff from the Los Angeles LGBT Center paired with a local organization to go door-to-door. More than fifty canvassers spoke to more than five hundred voters.

The conversations were tough. Raw and fraught with emotion. People against the legislation weren't just casually opposed, they had strongly held opinions based on religion, culture, and how they had been brought up. Not the easiest audience to convert.

But when researchers tabulated the results, they found something striking. A single ten-minute "deep canvassing" conversation made voters significantly more accepting. They had more positive feelings toward transgender people and were more supportive of laws protecting them from discrimination.

And the effect wasn't just short-lived. It persisted months after the canvassers had stopped by. It even withstood exposure to attack ads from the opposition.

The notion that one conversation can durably change minds about a controversial issue is heartening—amazing, even. But it brings up an even more important question: Why were these conversations so effective?

Conventional canvassing is a lot like being a mailman. Drop off the information, then on to the next house. Canvassers want to get in and out as quickly as possible.

You can see this in how canvassers practice. A group of trainees will divide in half, form two lines, and pair up. One will pretend they're the canvasser and one will pretend they're the voter. And the winner? The canvasser who is the briefest.

Deep canvassing takes longer. The goal, first and foremost, is to get the voter to be honest. To have a frank, candid interaction about a complex and often emotionally charged issue. And that's not happening in a couple minutes.

Dave Fleischer's team is willing to invest whatever time it takes to connect. To show that voter that it's safe for them to say whatever they feel. Whether they think the canvasser will like it or not.

That's why Virginia, in that jarring conversation with Gustavo, didn't get angry, didn't leave, and didn't jump on Gustavo when he used a blatant slur.[19]

"In South America we don't like fags," Gustavo had said.

And Virginia responded without raising her voice.

"Is that what you refer to as transgender or all gay people?" Virginia asked politely.

"Be whatever you are or whatever God made you . . . Don't try to be something else," Gustavo explained.

"So, for me, so I'm gay," said Virginia in a positive, upbeat tone.

"You're gay?" replied Gustavo. "Oh, my."

Rather than lecture Gustavo, Virginia began to tell her story. And Gustavo became interested. He asked Virginia what led her to make that "decision." Virginia explained that it wasn't a choice or a decision. It's just who she is. And they started to have a real conversation.

Virginia talked about how much she loves her partner, and this led Gustavo to talk about his own spouse. How his wife is disabled, and the challenges of bathing, feeding, and doing everything else for her. "God gave me the ability to love a disabled person," he explained, "and love is what really matters in the end."

"That resonates a lot with me," Virginia replied. "For me, these laws, and including transgender people, are about that. They're about how we treat one another."

Now that they had connected at a deeper level, Virginia circled back to the bathroom discussion. Virginia asked Gustavo what he thought was the worst thing that would happen if he and a transgender person used the bathroom at the same time. He shrugged. Nothing really, he admitted.

"Does it scare you?" Virginia asked.

"No," said Gustavo, readily indicating he wouldn't be worried.

Virginia had moved the discussion about bathrooms from some abstract hypothetical fear to something grounded in practical reality.

"Listen, probably I was mistaken," Gustavo said of his original transgender rights position.

"Would you vote in favor of banning transgender discrimination?" Virginia asked.

"In favor," Gustavo replied.

Virginia had switched the field. She had found an unsticking point.

Traditionally, when people think about taking another's perspective, it usually involves putting themselves "in someone else's shoes." Getting out of their own heads to see something from someone else's eyes.[20]

This works well when people can easily imagine what that other perspective is like. Say you're a high school student asked to help a struggling classmate by taking their perspective. If you've had academic challenges yourself, it's a useful exercise. You think back to the time you struggled with calculus, remember how you felt, and you use that to help understand your peer.

But what if you're a straight-A student? Well, then it's a much harder perspective to take. If you've always done well, it's hard to imagine what it's like to struggle academically. Which means trying to take another person's perspective won't really help you understand their emotional state.[21]

To avoid this issue, rather than inhabiting someone else's shoes, deep canvassing encourages voters to find a parallel situation from *their own* experience. Not imagining what it's like to *be* someone else, but a time the voter *felt similarly*.

A straight-A student may have a tough time understanding what it's like to struggle academically, but they've probably struggled at some point in their life. Whether in sports, dating, or some other domain, thinking about how that felt will help them better understand what someone struggling academically is going through.

Deep canvassing uses this to reduce prejudice. It's hard to imagine what life is like for someone else. Particularly if that person is a different race, gender, or sexual orientation.

You can ask most forty-five-year-old white men to imagine what it's like to be discriminated against, but they're unlikely to truly get it. Even if they try to take the perspective of a person who has been discriminated against, they've probably never wondered whether a waiter was rude to them because of their race or whether they were passed over for a promotion because of their gender.

So rather than asking voters to imagine what it's like to be transgendered, canvassers asked voters to find analogous experiences in their own lives. Virginia built on Gustavo's love for his disabled wife to help him see how she felt about her partner.

Other canvassers asked voters to think about a time they were judged negatively for being different. Then, once the voters shared their stories, canvassers encouraged them to see how their own experiences might offer a window into what transgender people are going through.

A military veteran talked about how companies didn't want to hire him because he had post-traumatic stress disorder. This was only one aspect of who he was, but potential employers couldn't see beyond it. The story wasn't about being transgender, but it helped him understand, and connect with, what it might be like for a transgender person to feel discriminated against because of that aspect of their identity.

Deep canvassing works because it switches the field. Rather than starting with the contentious issue, or the field on which people are far apart, it finds a dimension where people are closer together. Where they agree rather than disagree. An *unsticking point*.

When asked about transgender rights, abortion, or any other complex politically laden topic, it's easy to shoot things down that fall too far away. Staunch conservatives are sitting on their own ten-yard line, and transgender rights are clearly in the region of rejection, all the way on the liberal half of the field.

But deep canvassing changes the conversation. It's no longer an abstract debate about how someone thinks they should feel. It's not even about transgender rights. At least, not directly.

Instead, it's about love and adversity. About caring. Or about how it feels to be ostracized. To be judged negatively or discriminated against for being different. Something anyone can relate to, regardless of how they feel about this particular issue.

Rather than starting with a tough issue that seems divisive (a sticking point), deep canvassing starts with common ground. Something everyone can rally around.

Then, only after building that connection, do canvassers ultimately bend around and pivot to transgender rights.* Switching the playing field from one where two teams are dug in on different ends to one where everyone is on the same team.

Who would disagree about the importance of meaningful love? About reducing adversity and helping the ones we care about? And if you agree with those things, well, you might not have realized it, but protecting transgender rights is pretty close to something you already believe.

As Dave put it, "I know what I'm like when I'm my best self. I know what I'm like when I'm my worst self. And I appreciate when other people help me be my best self. That's what we're doing at the door. We're essentially saying, 'Hey, I see you. I see what you're like as your best self.' Is that how you see it? Is that how you want to be? If it is, how are you going to apply that thinking to your next vote?"

Deep canvassing had more than just a small effect. The impact was sizable. While the conversation was relatively brief, its effect

---

* If some of this sounds familiar, it should. Deep canvassing has a lot in common with the stairway model that hostage negotiators often use. Rather than jumping to trying to persuade, starting with something else and building trust and understanding. But instead of just starting with understanding, deep canvassing is about finding a place of agreement (an unsticking point) and then using that to switch the field to the dimension where things seem farther apart.

was larger than the change in attitudes toward gays and lesbians in the United States between 1998 and 2012. An almost fifteen-year period.

Most interesting, though, was whose minds were changed. It wasn't just the movable middle, Democrats who shifted a little bit, or people who already supported transgender rights. Deep canvassing worked equally well regardless of political affiliation or preexisting beliefs. It even convinced people initially opposed to transgender rights to warm to the issue.

Have a boss who doesn't support an initiative because they think it will cost too much? Dealing with a colleague who doesn't believe in company culture because they think it's too "squishy"? Catalysts switch the field and find an unsticking point.

Rather than pushing harder down the same blocked path, explore related directions where people aren't so dug in. Even though someone might seem like an adversary on one dimension, there's probably more to them than just that. Points of agreement like making sure the company continues to grow or employee retention stays high. Start with that. Start with the areas of agreement and build from there.

Distance is the third main roadblock to change. Reactance highlights that people push back when they feel someone is trying to persuade them. But even when just providing information or evidence, distance matters. If things are too far from where people are currently, they fall in the region of rejection and get discounted or ignored.

To catalyze change, then, we need to start by finding the movable middle. People for whom the change is not as large, and who can be used to help convince others. When trying to change those who are further away, we need to start by asking for less, as Dr. Priest did. Take big change and break it down into smaller, more manageable chunks or stepping-stones. Ask for less before asking for more. And finally, like Dave Fleischer's deep canvassers, we need to find an unsticking point. Start with a place of agreement and pivot from there to switch the field. Connecting to these parallel directions should move them enough to see the initial topic differently.

And maybe even change a little.

How to Change a Voter's Mind

What leads a lifelong Democrat to start voting Republican? A committed conservative to swing liberal?

So far, we've seen several examples of how shrinking distance can be used to drive political change. From getting conservatives to support transgender rights to encouraging prohibition supporters to consider loosening restrictions on booze.

But one could argue these are still rather small in scale. It's one thing to change opinions on a single issue (e.g., prohibition), but quite another to change political beliefs as a whole (i.e., switching political parties).

There are certainly famous examples of changing party affiliations. President Ronald Reagan was originally a Democrat, even head of a labor union, until 1962, when he became a member of the Republican Party. Senator Elizabeth Warren was a diehard conservative for years before becoming the progressive Democrat she is today.

But how does this work with everyday people? Is it possible to swing a voter? And if so, how?

Shifting from Right to Left

Silvia Branscom was born and raised in Enid, Oklahoma, in the mid-1970s. Nicknamed the Wheat Capital of Oklahoma, the town sits on the eastern edge of the Great Plains and is squarely in the heartland of America. Overwhelmingly white, the community is proudly "God-fearing," and Silvia started going to a Baptist church after her parents divorced when she was four years old.

Her mother eventually remarried, and Silvia's new stepfather was incredibly kind. He was a family man and treated her like she was his own flesh and blood. He taught Silvia about cars and how to do home repairs.

Politically, though, her stepfather was about as far right as could be. He was once part of the National Guard and vehemently protected people's right to bear arms. He believed in working hard and not accepting handouts. He was against abortion and believed women shouldn't be leaders.

Growing up, everyone loved Ronald Reagan, and Silvia did too. To be anything but conservative was to put your faith in God into question. How can you be a "baby killer"? When she was finally old enough to vote in a real election, Silvia voted "straight-ticket" Republican.

All the while, Silvia's own personal life was rushing forward. She did the typical small-town thing and got married right out of high school. By twenty-one she was pregnant. Every Sunday she and her husband went to church.

Silvia's husband was the head of the house, the breadwinner. She stayed at home and took care of the baby. She believed, and even said aloud, that "women should submit to their husbands." Eventually he graduated from college with a master's in petroleum engineering, and the family moved to Alaska.

Silvia had always wanted to go back to school. She loved learning and was even getting a liberal arts degree at a junior college before her pregnancy forced her to stop taking classes. The move reignited her interest, and she started taking two classes a semester at the University of Alaska.

At the university, she had two influential professors. Two faculty members who started to change her mind.

One was in her debate class. He made the claim that there was no such thing as universal truth. She argued back that God was a universal truth.

Then the class had a debate on the Second Amendment. The right to bear arms. In Silvia's mind it was an easy win and she enthusiastically volunteered to defend it.

She got obliterated. Completely and utterly destroyed. She was up against another student who was a national debate competitor, ranked fourth in the nation. Silvia had never heard any of the arguments her classmate brought forward. Back home, to question was to be shunned.

Another influential professor taught her class on Western civilization. Silvia had been raised to believe that those who were not Christian either had never heard about Christ or were bad people who did drugs and committed crimes. Her professor debunked all that. He wasn't Christian, but he was kind and a good citizen and knew the Bible better than anyone she had ever met. Better than all the Christians back in Oklahoma.

He taught the class all about the Crusades and various forms of Christian oppression. All of which had been framed much differently back home.

Neither professor tried to convince Silvia that her beliefs were wrong or pushed her to believe that theirs were right. They didn't tell her what to do or how to think. They simply showed her that there was another path. That there was a different approach.

The Western civilization professor, in particular, was similar enough to Silvia to fall within the zone of acceptance but different enough to encourage her to shift. He knew the Bible inside and out; he just had a different perspective on it.

Silvia was still a Republican and a devout Christian, but she started to have questions. She began to struggle with beliefs she had long taken for granted.

Then her husband was transferred to Scotland. Silvia couldn't finish her bachelor's, but she was exposed to a world she had never seen before.

In the UK Silvia met a Muslim person for the first time. A woman whose son went to the same nursery school. Later Silvia befriended a woman from India. She started to become more global in her thinking.

Things started to seem murky. The religious beliefs that appeared so obvious before, or the answers that she had once been told were right, suddenly didn't seem so straightforward.

When Silvia eventually returned to the United States, things looked different. She was struck by the lack of interest in prioritizing education. She used to be a massive sports fan, but now all the money funneled into sports instead of education just seemed offensive. Teachers in Oklahoma had to strike because they were paid less than $40,000 per year while the local high school spent $400,000 re-turfing their football field.

She was surprised to discover so much gun violence and systemic racism, especially within the criminal justice system. Having given birth to her daughter in England, she was appalled at the lack of health care. Even the sermons at church didn't seem quite right. All the talk about love and kindness extended only to others of the same faith.

Ultimately, it took her almost ten years to change. She had voted for George H. W. Bush in 1992 and Bob Dole in 1996. Eventually she felt that the Republican Party no longer reflected her values. The party said they cared about faith but didn't share her concern for the weak and marginalized.

In 2000 she voted for Al Gore.

Today, Silvia considers herself a Democrat. She believes in racial and gender equality and that society is better for everyone when everyone is looked after.

It saddens her that America is so divided. She doesn't have the anger toward Republicans that many Democrats do, and she believes that most Republican citizens mean well, but she is repelled by most Republican politicians and the way they use fear to get elected. Rural communities are all about church and family. Sometimes they forget that we are all one family and worthy of being taken care of.

Shifting from Left to Right

Diego Martinez grew up in California's Central Valley. Modesto, to be exact. Ninety miles east of San Francisco, the blue-collar city is home to the world's largest winery. The fertile farmland of the surrounding areas grows almonds, walnuts, and a variety of other crops. Over a third of residents identify as Hispanic or Latino, and while not as liberal as the rest of California, the area skews more liberal than conservative.

Diego's parents emigrated from Mexico and he studied at Modesto Junior College before transferring to San Diego State.

When Diego first registered to vote, like many of his friends he registered as a Democrat. The hot topics were marriage equality, helping the less fortunate, and staying out of foreign wars. Democrats also seemed to be more friendly toward immigrants. All of which were important things to Diego, and he voted Democrat again and again. For Obama in both 2008 and 2012 and Hillary in 2016.

But toward the end of 2016, Diego started to become bothered by what the Democratic Party stood for. He found Obama's comments about the pay gap between men and women to be concerning. Diego agreed there was a gap, just not for the reasons Obama outlined. And Diego was troubled by what he saw as Obama becoming a "social justice" warrior.

He also didn't like the way Democrats he knew were behaving. Living in New York City at the time, he saw more and more of his Democratic friends adopting holier-than-thou attitudes toward others. Like they knew all the answers. Like their party could solve all the problems better than anyone else could.

But what bothered Diego the most was the lack of open discourse. Among his friends and peers, if you didn't wholly agree with the liberal Democratic consensus, then you must be a racist. A bigot. Or something like that. Democrats just seemed out of touch with the real world.

He felt like he was being pushed. And he didn't like it. So he started looking more broadly.

He started listening to Jordan Peterson, a psychology professor from the University of Toronto and a strong critic of political correctness. He started following Ben Shapiro, a conservative political commentator who wrote about how universities are indoctrinating America's youth. And he started paying attention to the work of Nassim Taleb. All within his zone of acceptance but slowly pulling him toward the other side of the field.

Diego found their points compelling. They were some of the most intelligent people he had ever listened to. And their ideas on topics like free speech, responsibility, self-actualization, and history made sense to him and slowly began to influence his thinking.

Taleb's work in particular helped Diego put into words something he had long felt about his Democratic friends. That they clamor for equality of the races but have never been out drinking with a Russian cabdriver. That they talk a lot about abstract lofty ideals but never actually touch things in reality.

He saw Democrats, and particularly his liberal peers, as fixated on things like diversity and equality rather than real and bigger problems such as the economy and national security. It blew his mind that the same liberal friends who pointed to science as proof that climate change exists were so quick to dismiss the idea that men and women are biologically different.

Diego began to see himself being drawn toward the more conservative end of the spectrum. And by summer 2017, Diego became a registered Republican.

Diego doesn't think that his Republican or conservative friends have gotten everything right. And he wasn't happy that Trump won. But the fact that so many liberals said they were devastated by Trump's victory? Diego felt that was a little too much. It's liberals engaging in more virtue signaling rather than buckling down and dealing with the real problems.

Diego knows the United States is more than just the coastal, rich, educated cities. He values the free speech he feels Republicans encourage. And while he's lost left-leaning friends because of ideological differences, he's never had a right-leaning friend call him a racist for disagreeing with them.

Silvia and Diego's stories might seem quite different. A Caucasian woman from the heartland of America who went from right to left. And a Hispanic man from the West Coast who went from left to right.

But while their journeys went in different directions, they actually have a lot in common. And not just that they grew up in regions rich in agriculture.

In both cases, a few key individuals helped shift their views. Not by telling them what to do or pushing them to change, but by reducing reactance. By allowing for agency. By guiding or shaping their journey and opening their eyes to new information and new ideas. College professors and public intellectuals, sure, but also regular friends they met through their daily lives.

Further, as with most big changes, things didn't happen right away. Someone had to shrink the distance. It took a number of small steps rather than one big leap. Multiple interactions over months or even years A slow, gradual change brought upon by getting a chance to see the world or being concerned about a lack of meaningful discourse.

By starting with things they had in common and building from there, the catalysts in Silvia's and Diego's lives changed their minds.

Beyond distance, though, there's another roadblock we have to wrestle with. And that is uncertainty.

4. Uncertainty

In 1998, former minor-league baseball ticket salesman Nick Swinmurn was crisscrossing back and forth through a San Francisco mall. He was searching for a pair of shoes. Not just any shoes. He wanted a certain type of Airwalk boots.

One store had the right style but the wrong color. Another store had the right color but the wrong size. An hour later Nick was still going from store to store, fruitlessly searching. After exhausting his options, he went home frustrated and empty-handed. *There must be a better way*, he thought.

The Internet craze had taken over the Bay Area, and Nick thought an online shoe store could work. All the brands, styles, sizes, and colors people wanted, all in one easy-to-search place. He raised some funding, put together a basic website, and Shoesite.com was born.

But building an online business was tough. And just a few months later, Shoesite.com was running out of cash. The business had burned through its first round of funding and was having trouble raising a second. Sales were sluggish and not high enough to impress the bigger venture firms.

Simply put, venture capitalists didn't want to invest in an online shoe company. From one firm to the next, the response was the same: Who would ever buy shoes on the Internet?

Shoesite.com's only salvation was that it didn't have any competition, because everyone thought it was a terrible business to be in.

Today we shop for everything online. Shoes and clothes, certainly, but also mortgages, cars, doctors, and even pets. For people who grew up swiping right to find dates, never knowing the alien sounds of a dial-up modem, it's hard to imagine a life in which anything you need isn't just a click away.

But it wasn't always that way. While the ubiquity of online shopping today makes it seem like its adoption was a quick, steep rise, the truth was far from that.

In fact, in the late 1990s and early 2000s, e-commerce was floundering. Despite all the hype and excitement, online sales made up only a sliver of all sales. Out of every hundred dollars of goods and services purchased, barely more than a nickel was done online. In fact, most online commerce was actually business-to-business transactions. Manufacturing shipments and wholesale goods.

Pets.com went from advertising during the Super Bowl to laying off all its employees. Grocery delivery company Webvan went from a billion-dollar valuation to shutting its doors eighteen months later. For a six-week period in October and November 2000, dot-coms were closing at a rate of around one a day.

Even Amazon was hurting. It lost $323 million in the last quarter of 1999 and in 2000 its stock finished the year down more than 83 percent from its fifty-two-week high.

The problem was that people were used to shopping in physical stores. Whenever they wanted something, they would get in their cars, drive to the nearest retailer, and pick through whatever happened to be on the shelves.

It might not have been the best way to shop, or the most efficient, but it was a habit. It was familiar and safe.

For Shoesite.com to succeed, Nick needed to change consumer behavior. He needed to overcome something called the uncertainty tax.

The Uncertainty Tax

A couple years ago I needed a break from the cold. The winter had been particularly tough, and the city was mired in frigid temperatures and polar vortexes. It was time for a vacation.

Miami seemed perfect. Even in February, temperatures were in the mid-seventies and sunny. It offered beautiful beaches and great food. All I needed to do was to find a hotel.

After searching different websites, I narrowed the choice to two options. Both had oceanfront rooms with balconies for about the same price.

The only difference was how nice the rooms were. Hotel A had been renovated a decade or two earlier and the rooms were in decent shape. Not amazing, but not terrible.

Hotel B had been partially fixed up more recently. Some of the rooms were completely remodeled and immaculate. They looked beautiful, with high-concept furniture and new rugs. The other rooms, however, hadn't been updated in a while. They looked dingy with outmoded fixtures and beds that were past their prime.

If I could get one of the better rooms at Hotel B, the choice would be easy. But when I called, the representative said it would depend on when other guests checked out. They could note my preference but made no guarantees.

I had a decision to make. Book Hotel A and get a pretty good room for sure, or take a gamble on Hotel B? Maybe something better, but maybe something worse.

If you were in a similar situation, what would you choose? The sure thing or the risky option with the chance of a higher upside?

Scientists haven't run this exact experiment, but they've run dozens if not hundreds like it. Give people a choice between a certain, good thing and an uncertain but potentially better thing and see what they pick.

Take a choice between $30 and a gamble: an 80 percent chance of getting $45 and a 20 percent chance of getting nothing.

Unlike my Miami hotel, here you can easily calculate a "right" answer, or what a completely rational person should do. The gamble has a higher expected return. Run it ten times and you should get $45 eight times out of ten. Sure, you'd get nothing a couple times, but most of the time you'd get more than the guaranteed $30.

And even considering the couple of times you get nothing, in expectation, the gamble is still a better bet. Do it ten times and you'd expect to net $8 \times \$45 = \$360$, while the sure thing would only give you $10 \times \$30 = \$300$.

But think about what you would do in this situation. Would you take the guaranteed $30 or go for the gamble?

If you're like most people, you probably said you would pick the sure thing. The guaranteed 30 bucks. Even though it has lower expected value and would net less money on average.

Why? Because people are risk averse. They like knowing what they are getting, and as long as what they are getting is positive, they prefer sure things to risky ones.* Even if the risky choice is better, on average.

It would be great to get a newly remodeled hotel room. My vacation would be that much more amazing because of it. But how frustrating would it be to end up in one of the older rooms? Even if the chance is relatively low, is it worth the risk?

This devaluing of things uncertain is called the "uncertainty tax." When choosing between a sure thing and a risky one, the risky option has to be that much better to get chosen. The remodeled room has to be that much nicer. The gamble has to be that much higher in expected value.

And the uncertainty tax is a lot larger than you might think.

In the early 2000s, three University of Chicago researchers asked people how much they would be willing to pay for a $50 gift card.[1] The gift card was to a local retailer and had to be used in the next two weeks.

After thinking about it, people said they would be willing to pay around $26 on average. Some didn't shop at that retailer, and

---

* Risk aversion is particularly true in the domain of gains, or getting something positive. In the domain of losses, people are actually risk seeking. Rather than lose a small amount of money for sure, they'd rather gamble and take a chance on losing a larger amount of money to also have the chance of not losing anything at all.

others might have been worried about the two-week expiration date. These aspects, combined with others, led them to value the gift card at around half its actual value.

Another group of people was asked how much they would be willing to pay for a $100 gift card to that retailer, and the results were similar. On average, people said they would pay around $45. Some said more, some said less, but on average, for all the reasons noted above, people said they would pay around half its actual value.

Again, no surprise.

For a third group, however, the researchers introduced some uncertainty.[2] This group was offered a lottery ticket with a fifty-fifty shot. A 50 percent chance of winning a $50 gift card and a 50 percent chance of winning a $100 gift card. How much would people pay for this lottery ticket?[3]

Before getting to the answer, consider an even simpler question. Compared to the $50 gift card, how much *should* people be willing to pay for the lottery ticket? Should they be willing to pay more than the $50 gift card? Less? About the same?

When thinking through a question like this, the "rational" answer is pretty clear-cut. The value of a risky opportunity should sit between the best and worst possible outcomes.

Take a used car. The blue book value is $10,000, but the car might need a new timing belt. And if it does, the repair would cost $1,000. Given that, most people would say the car's value is somewhere between $9,000 and $10,000. The value if it does or doesn't need the new belt.

You might average the two values and say the car is worth $9,500. Or lean more toward $9,000 (e.g., $9,250) if you really think it needs a new timing belt. Regardless, the used car's value should sit somewhere between $9,000 and $10,000. Somewhere between the best and worst possible outcome.

The same logic should apply to the gift cards. It's not clear whether the lottery ticket will net a $50 gift card or a $100 gift card, but worst case it's a $50 one. So people should be willing to pay at least that much. Maybe not a lot more, but at least a little.

But they weren't.

No. When researchers analyzed the data, they found the exact opposite. People weren't willing to pay more for the lottery ticket. Not even a little. And they weren't even willing to pay the same amount. In fact, while they were willing to pay around $26 for the $50 gift card and $45 for the $100 gift card, they were willing to pay only around $16 for the lottery ticket. Almost 50 percent less than even its worst possible outcome.[4]

And the reason why is the uncertainty tax.

People bidding on the gift cards knew exactly what they were going to get. They would exchange a certain amount of money for a gift card of a certain amount.

But people buying the lottery ticket didn't have that certainty. They didn't know which outcome was going to happen. And even though both outcomes were decent, that uncertainty was costly. Which made them value the ticket less.

Change almost always involves some degree of uncertainty. Is buying shoes online a good idea? Will it save me time and effort or be a bigger hassle? Will the shoes fit? Will I like how they look? It's hard to know for sure.

And people dislike uncertainty. Not just a little, like bad weather or spoiled milk or a host of other things they find mildly annoying. No, people *really* dislike uncertainty. So much so that it has a real, tangible cost.

Uncertainty is even worse than certain negative outcomes. Knowing you'll be late to a meeting certainly feels bad, but wondering whether you'll make it on time usually feels worse. Getting fired isn't fun, but wondering if you're about to be fired is worse still.

Consequently, the more change involves uncertainty, the less interested people are in changing. The more ambiguity there is around a product, service, or idea, the less valuable that thing becomes. Less like a gift card and more like a lottery ticket.

Not sure whether a lawn care company can fix those brown spots in the yard? Might as well just skip it. Unclear whether management will reward people for "thinking outside the box"? Might as well not rock the boat and keep doing things the way they've always been done.

Uncertainty undermines the value of doing things differently, making it less likely people will change.

And if decreasing the value of new things weren't enough, uncertainty creates yet another roadblock. It often halts decision-making entirely.

Hitting the Pause Button

In a famous study, researchers asked Stanford students to imagine they had just taken a tough qualifying exam.[5]

It is the end of the semester, you feel tired and run-down, and you find out that you passed the exam. You now have the opportunity to buy a very attractive 5-day Christmas vacation package to Hawaii

*at an exceptionally low price. The special offer expires tomorrow.
Would you*

> *(a) Buy the vacation package?*
> *(b) Not buy the vacation package?*
> *(c) Pay a $5 nonrefundable fee in order to retain the right to buy
> the vacation package at the same exceptional price the day
> after tomorrow?*

The first two options are straightforward. Buy the trip or
don't. The third involves deferring choice. Rather than taking
action, suspending judgment and putting the choice or action off
until later.

Most students said they would buy the vacation package.
Some said they wouldn't, and some said they would defer the
choice until later, but the majority said they would go for it.

A second group of students received a similar scenario, except
they were told that they had failed. That they would have to take
the exam again in a couple months after the holidays.

Even though these "failers" hadn't passed, their choices were
almost identical to those who had. Most said they would buy the
vacation package.

This makes sense. Pass the exam, and the vacation becomes a
reward. Go to Hawaii to celebrate! Fail the exam, and, well, the
vacation becomes a consolation prize. A chance to rest and recu-
perate before taking the exam again. Two different reasons, the
same choice in the end.

But there was also a third group of participants. Rather than
being told whether they had passed or failed, these students were
told that the results were still up in the air. That the outcome of
the exam was uncertain. And, just like the "failers," they were

told that if they failed, they would have to retake the exam in a couple months.

If people would go on vacation if they passed and go on vacation if they failed, then not knowing whether they passed or failed shouldn't matter. Even if they're uncertain about the outcome of the exam, they should still go on vacation.

But adding uncertainty changed what people chose. Rather than buying the vacation package, most people decided to defer choice and wait until things became more certain. They decided to do nothing rather than move forward.

In this way, uncertainty acts like a pause button. Stopping action and freezing things where they are.

So, while uncertainty is great for the status quo, or whatever people were doing before, it's terrible for changing minds. Because rather than moving ahead and doing something new, uncertainty makes people wait and stick with whatever they have always been doing. At least until that uncertainty resolves. If it ever does.

Uncertain about whether online shopping will be better? Might as well just drive to the store like you've done in the past. Not sure if a new project is really worth staffing? Might as well defer making a choice until things become more certain.

New things almost always involve uncertainty, so if it's not clear how much better something new will be, might as well play it safe and stick with the status quo.

Like a caution flag at the speedway or a construction sign on the highway, uncertainty slows forward progress.[6] It makes people pause and take their foot off the gas.

So how can we get people to un-pause?

Trialability

It turns out that the answer to this question comes from what might seem like a totally unrelated domain: hybrid corn.

Everett Rogers was born on a family farm in rural Iowa in the early 1930s. The Great Depression had just begun, and while life was tough everywhere, there were few places where it was tougher than rural Iowa. The farm had no heat, internal plumbing, or electricity, and from a young age Rogers had to do his share to keep the farm afloat. He divided his time between going to class in a one-room schoolhouse and feeding chickens, milking cows, and doing whatever other chores were needed.

College wasn't the first thing on his mind, and Rogers would have stayed home had a teacher not filled his car with promising seniors and driven them to look at Iowa State. Rogers had never been to the university, but he liked what he saw and decided to pursue a degree in agriculture.

Every summer Rogers would come back to work on the family farm and bring back information about the latest and greatest farming innovations. New insights about the benefits of crop rotation or technologies that could increase efficiency and yield.

For the most part, though, people ignored his advice. Rogers's dad was reluctant to adopt hybrid seed corn, for example, even though it was bred to be drought-resistant and to have a 25 percent higher yield.

Rogers wondered why. So, after getting a master's, he returned to Iowa State to do a PhD.

A few years earlier, two faculty members had examined exactly the innovation Rogers's father had ignored: hybrid corn. Surveying more than 250 farmers in two Iowa communities, they found that even although hybrid corn was technically "better" (i.e., had stronger stalks and produced more corn per seed), it took thirteen years until everyone finally adopted it. And even when farmers started using the new seed, it took them almost a decade to use it for their entire crop.

Rogers was fascinated. He decided to do a similar study on weed spray.

While doing background reading, he came across research from other disciplines that had begun to look at similar questions. What impacts the spread of education programs or the success of a new pharmaceutical drug.

Rogers saw similarities across these various areas and began to formulate a general "diffusion" model. A theory about not just agricultural innovations and farmers but what would make any new invention, technology, or idea diffuse through any population. Whether that population was made up of consumers, employees, teachers, or anyone else.

When he presented this model to his dissertation committee, though, they were skeptical. How could the same reasons drive success across different innovations, people, places, and cultures? The very notion seemed ridiculous.

As Rogers walked out of the building later that day, he happened to run into one of his committee members. The professor was engrossed in reading a book, but he glanced up briefly as Rogers passed by. "Your committee had many questions about how generalizable your diffusion model is," said the professor, "but maybe you could have an interesting book."

Decades later, Rogers's book *Diffusion of Innovations* is a modern classic. It's the second-most cited social science book, referenced almost 100,000 times in everything from marketing and management to engineering, economics, and energy policy.

In it, Rogers argues that up to 87 percent of the variance in how quickly things are adopted can be explained by just five attributes. Looking across such diverse things as hybrid corn and modern math to refrigerators and, in more recent editions, the advent of the Internet, Rogers suggested that a handful of features explained why some things become big hits and others are slow to gain traction.

And of the key factors Rogers identified, the most important, the one that explained the most variance in the studies he reviewed, was a concept he called "trialability."

Simply put, trialability is how easy it is to try something. The ease with which something can be tested or experimented with on a limited basis.

Some products, services, or ideas are easy to try. If someone tells you about a new blog, for example, and sends you a link, it's relatively effortless to check out. With one click you're on the site and can get a sense of what it covers, what it's like, and whether it's something you'd be interested in.

Same with a new brand of paper towels. They're cheap, easy to find, and don't require any additional learning to use.

Contrast that with a new type of practice management software for financial advisors. If an advisor has to purchase the software, spend hours entering information, and then get all their clients to sign up and do the same—all before learning whether the software actually saves time or money—it's not very easy to try.

The easier it is to try something, the more people will use it, and the faster it catches on.[7] Drug treatment programs that participated in a drug trial were five times more likely to eventually adopt that medication. Whether university lecturers adopted new teaching technologies depended heavily on whether they could try them out beforehand. And dozens of other studies looking at everything from internet banking and cloud computing to farming innovations and computer games found that trialability is a large and significant driver of adoption.

Trialability works because making things easier to try lowers uncertainty. It makes it easier for people to experience and evaluate new things.

But trialability doesn't have to be fixed. Yes, certain products, services, initiatives, and ideas tend to be easier to try than others, but even within the *same* thing there are ways to increase trialability. Ways to change people's minds, to get them to un-pause. To support, do, buy, or try something new.

The question, then, is how to reduce uncertainty by lowering the barrier to trial. Four key ways to do that are to (1) harness freemium, (2) reduce up-front costs, (3) drive discovery, and (4) make it reversible.[8]

Harness Freemium

Like Uber and Airbnb, Dropbox often appears on lists of "unicorns," or privately held start-ups with valuations of more than $1 billion. In less than a decade, the file hosting company has amassed more than 500 million registered users. More than 200,000 businesses and organizations have signed up, and the company is valued at more than $10 billion.

But it wasn't always that way.

At the outset, Dropbox struggled to get customers to sign up. The technology was innovative, but they were trying to solve a problem most people didn't realize they had. Everyone was used to storing files and pictures and other content on their PCs, and switching to a cloud-based service seemed a bit daunting. After pouring hours into a perfect document, the last thing you want to worry about is that it will disappear. Same with cherished family photos. Seeing something on your desktop provided a sense of security, but the cloud was more nebulous and difficult to understand. Sure, Dropbox offered more space and easy access, but what if the servers went down?

Dropbox's CEO thought about hiring a marketing person or buying some search ads, but the firm didn't have a lot of money to spend, and the return on investment seemed low. So, rather than trying to convince people how great their service was, Dropbox did something else.

They gave it away for free.

On the surface, this might seem backward. Give your product away for free? This seems to violate the basic laws of successful business. Even an eight-year-old with a lemonade stand knows that to make money, you have to charge. Why would a company that wants to be profitable give their product or service away for nothing?

But it worked.

In just two months, the number of users more than doubled. In less than a year, the number had increased tenfold. And soon Dropbox was making billions of dollars in revenue.

Dropbox grew by harnessing a business model called freemium. Sign up and you can start using the service for free. You can store your files, upload photos, and try a variety of other features, all without having to pay the firm a penny.

It's obvious why customers like freemium. Who doesn't like free stuff?

But freemium can be just as valuable for the company itself. Because making the service free encouraged more people to try it.

Someone might have heard about Dropbox, and even thought about using it, but if they have to pay $20, $10, or even $5 for the privilege, they might say no, thanks. After all, learning something new already takes effort. Add a monthly fee on top of that, and unless people are dissatisfied with their current solution, the costs of change become just too much to bear.

Making Dropbox free to try, however, reduces those costs a bit. Sure, people still have to upload all their files and learn a new system, but the fact that the service is free initially encourages more of them to sign up and take a look.

If that was all freemium did, though, it wouldn't be enough. Acquiring new customers is great, but eventually the company has to make money.

And that's where the second part comes in.

"Freemium" is a portmanteau, a linguistic blend of two words: "free" and "premium." The initial or basic version is free of charge, but the experience is designed so that satisfied users will eventually pay to upgrade to an enhanced or premium version.

Dropbox provides a decent amount of free storage. Enough to share big documents, upload PowerPoint presentations, and start saving photos and videos.

And once people start using Dropbox, it becomes a habit. While they might have previously used a pile of memory sticks or an external hard drive, the free space is enough to get them using Dropbox instead. It becomes their go-to way to share files, host group projects, or save cherished memories.

But building that habit takes space. And eventually people who store lots of things end up running out of free storage. So, to get more space or gain access to additional features, they upgrade to the paid version.*

Freemium gives users the time and space to explore what the service has to offer. Sure, some people might upload one file and that's the end of it, but if the service is useful, people will come back a second time and a third. And in so doing, they'll realize the value the service provides.

Rather than having to convince people how great Dropbox is, users convince themselves. Because they've already been using it and loving it.

Dropbox isn't alone. Hundreds of companies have used freemium to drive success. Playing Candy Crush is free, but unlocking certain levels or features requires paying a nominal fee. Reading the *New York Times* online is free initially, but once

---

* Freemium often takes advantage of so-called switching costs. Given the time and energy it takes to start using Dropbox, once you've loaded a bunch of your files, you're less likely to switch to a competitor. Even if that competitor is offering twice as much free space. In this way, freemium is similar to a razor–razorblade pricing model (although in that case the initial period is not free). Companies often give away razors or sell them quite cheaply in the hope of locking consumers into their proprietary system or platform. Different companies' razorblades often fit only their own razors, so once someone is using one system, they are locked in, which allows the company to then charge a premium for the razorblades. As King Camp Gillette, founder of the company that bears his name, once said: "Give 'em the razor; sell 'em the blades." Hardware-software pairings often work the same way. A new video game system will be sold at cost, or even at a loss, because the company knows they can recoup their investment by making a profit later on through selling games that run only on their system.

you've read ten articles in a given month, you have to pay to read more. Pandora, Skype, LinkedIn, Evite, Spotify, SurveyMonkey, WordPress, and Evernote are just a handful of the companies that have thrived using this approach.[9]

Importantly, Freemium isn't about tricking people. Dropbox doesn't say the service is free to start, only to surprise them later with a monthly fee. There's no bait and switch.

People only get charged if and when they decide they want an upgrade. When they want more storage, extra features, or additional functionality, they make the choice.

When freemium works, it encourages upgrading without requiring it. Similar to the idea of allowing for autonomy that we discussed in the Reactance chapter, letting people choose if and when they want to move from the free version to the paid one.

If Dropbox asked people to pay for storage right away, or companies like Pandora asked people to pay for an ad-free version, most potential users would likely say no. They wouldn't be certain that it was worth paying for. But because the freemium version helps people discover the value of the service—and, in Pandora's case, the annoyance of ads—they're much happier to fork over a few bucks.*

Not everyone pays to upgrade, but more people trying the

---

* Freemium works best when the customer understands why the paid version has to cost money. Storage is relatively easy to understand. While the "cloud" makes it seem like the files are just suspended in air, most people recognize that they are being hosted on some server somewhere that someone has to pay for. Just as it costs money to keep a bunch of boxes in a self-storage unit, storing files has a cost. When the additional features don't clearly require an incremental cost, articulating the value that comes with the paid services becomes even more important.

service initially increases the chance that more people become paid users later on. Trying before buying makes people more likely to buy.

See the Applying Freemium appendix for more detail on how to apply a freemium business model.

Reducing Up-front Costs

Freemium is particularly useful for digital goods and services. Situations where an offering can easily be changed, seamlessly upgrading users from a basic version to a paid one.

But the same ideas can be applied more broadly. And to demonstrate how, it helps to examine how Nick Swinmurn resolved his challenges with Shoesite.com.

After getting turned down by yet another venture capitalist, Shoesite.com founder Nick Swinmurn met with executive Fred Mossler to brainstorm next steps. They needed to come up with a way to jump-start sales—and quickly; otherwise Shoesite.com would soon be out of business.

One idea they discussed was discounting. Cut prices to encourage customers to buy. Some of the larger e-commerce businesses like eBay and Amazon had reputations for dropping prices to drive new customer and revenue growth.

But Nick and Fred were worried this wouldn't sit well with their partners. Shoe companies are relentless about protecting brand equity. Consumers are willing to pay more for Nikes because they think Nike is a cool, premium brand. Discounting might erode that equity. So footwear brands avoided partners that dropped prices.

Further, while discounting might attract some customers in the short term, it wouldn't change the fundamental issue: people were wary of shopping online. Discounting would only be a Band-Aid. And an ineffective one at that.

So, Nick and team came up with a different approach. No one they knew was doing anything similar, and they weren't clear whether it made sense businesswise, but it was certainly novel: free shipping.

At the time, free shipping was a big risk. Nick and Fred had no idea if it would work or how much it would cost to implement.

Back then, most e-commerce companies looked at shipping as a profit center. A place to pad margins a bit and make a buck or two on "shipping and handling."

Free shipping meant that rather than making money on shipping, Shoesite.com would be losing it. Every time a customer ordered something, Shoesite.com would have to pay to get it there. Summed across customers, this would soon become a significant cost. Further, Shoesite.com would have to manage excess inventory and deal with all the merchandise customers sent back.

But Shoesite.com was out of options. They were running out of money fast and didn't have time to test or explore.

So Nick and Fred gave it a shot. In November 1999, they announced free shipping on top of the company's web page.

Nothing happened. Not immediately, at least.

But soon sales started growing. By 2001, Shoesite.com had a few million dollars in revenue, and just three years later they were doing more than twenty times that. Skip ahead a few years and the company was selling more than a billion dollars in merchandise a year.

Today their warehouses boast more than 3.2 million items from almost a thousand brands. Shoes, of course, but also a range of clothes, jewelry, accessories, and even luggage. In fact, even if you haven't bought something from them, you probably know at least a couple of people who have.

Never heard of Shoesite.com?

Maybe you're more familiar with the name the company changed to a few months after its launch. An adaptation of *zapatos*, the Spanish word for shoes. Or, as you might know the company today, Zappos.

When it launched free shipping, Zappos got a lot of pushback. No one thought it would succeed, and it was an expensive gambit.

But it worked because it removed the main barrier to purchase. It reduced uncertainty.

Nick and Fred knew customers weren't comfortable shopping online because they wanted to try shoes on. Unlike traditional retail, where customers can touch and feel before purchase, shopping online meant paying up-front. Shelling out money before experiencing the product, knowing whether it worked, or, in the case of shoes, if they fit. And if people can't try before they buy, it's hard for them to be sure they'll like what they end up with.

This uncertainty was preventing people from buying online. And they didn't want to have to pay a shipping charge to reduce it.

"If we could remove that," Fred said, "we could create the

mental picture of bringing the shoe store into your own home. Order as many as you wanted, try them all on, send back what you didn't want."

And that's what customers did (and do today). People order two, three, or even ten pairs of shoes, try them on, keep the winners, and return the duds. Customer service reps are even instructed to encourage customers to order two sizes of shoes to make sure they end up with a pair that fits.

Do all those people ordering extra shoes cost Zappos money? Certainly.

But over time what proved out was that the average order size increased. Not just from customers buying more and returning them, but from keeping more pairs, just as they would from shopping at a regular store. People were comfortable ordering more because they could freely return them.

Beyond Zappos, though, free shipping was the catalyst that made e-commerce into the behemoth it is today: Just think about Amazon Prime.[10] Success came not from dropping prices, or devising a clever slogan, but by removing the roadblock that was hindering change.

By allowing consumers to experience things like they would in a physical store, without having to pay for the opportunity, free shipping overcame the uncertainty tax and changed how people shop forever.

When considering examples like freemium and Zappos, it's easy to think the common denominator is one word: "free." It might seem like lowering the barrier to trial is all about money. About making things cheaper or, better yet, free.

But money isn't the only or even largest barrier to change. A free shipping offer that saves $5.99, for example, is more appealing to many customers than a discount that cuts the item's price by $10.[11]

Because the real barrier isn't money; it's uncertainty: Will I like the shoes? Will they even fit?

Dropping the price by $10 helps on the money front, but it doesn't reduce the uncertainty. The product is cheaper, but it doesn't provide any better sense of whether I'll like the shoes or whether they'll fit.

And having to pay to get the opportunity to resolve that uncertainty only makes people less likely to act. They might as well hit pause and do nothing instead.

Imagine you couldn't test drive a car before you bought it. Having to pay tens of thousands of dollars before knowing whether you liked the handling or were comfortable in the front seat would make you much less likely to switch from your existing car and buy anything new.

Test drives, whether at the car dealership or at the Apple store with a new tech gadget, give people a sense of what something is like before they have to commit. It doesn't make the car any cheaper if they end up buying it, but it reduces uncertainty about whether buying it is a good idea in the first place.

That's why "online-only" retailers like Casper Sleep (mattresses) and Warby Parker (prescription glasses) started opening physical stores. Casper built a business on eschewing traditional retail and only selling online. It helped cut costs and kept prices down.

But some potential customers still wanted to sit on a mattress before ordering it. So Casper built a "napmobile" that drove around the country, opened pop-up stores, and eventually created permanent locations where people could test out the beds.*

Pilots give television executives a lower-cost way to see how a show performs. Renting gives potential buyers a lower-cost way to check out a neighborhood and potential skiers a chance to try the sport before having to buy all the gear. The item still costs the same if people buy it, but renting makes it easier for them to try before they buy.[12]

Marine clothing company Guy Cotten even used this concept to get people to use life jackets.

Everyone knows they should wear one while boating, but many people still don't. So, to help people see why life jackets are so vital, the company lowered the up-front cost. They couldn't give out samples, and mailing life jackets for free would get expensive, so instead they created Sortie en Mer, a first-person online drowning simulator.

Shot in a first-person perspective, the simulator shows a beautiful day on a sailboat. You're having fun on the water, talking to your friend—but not wearing a life jacket. Suddenly a swinging mast knocks you into the water. Your friend tries to turn the sailboat around to get you, but the wind picks up and the boat gets carried away, leaving you stuck treading water.

---

* Dividing big things into smaller chunks is also useful. Having to sign a full-year contract may scare some people away, so gyms now allow people to go month to month. Large multinationals wanted to sell to rural India, but most consumers couldn't afford the regular prices. So the companies started offering smaller sizes. Rather than 700 milliliters of Head & Shoulders, consumers could get 10 milliliters for only 5 rupees (about 7 cents). This so-called sachet revolution enabled consumers to try a range of products, and now almost every fast-moving consumer good is offered this way.

And the only way to stay afloat, to keep yourself from drowning, is to scroll with your mouse without stopping.

Scrolling your mouse sounds like no big deal, even fun for few seconds. But soon it becomes exhausting. So people give up. And when they stop scrolling, they see themselves slowly sinking to the bottom of the ocean.

The experience is creepy, to be sure, but that's exactly the point. Think scrolling for a couple minutes is tough? Imagine what trying to tread water for hours would be like. Might be worth wearing a life vest.

These and similar examples work by reducing the up-front cost.[13] They shrink the amount of time, money, or effort required at the outset to experience something. Free shipping avoids charging customers for the privilege of trying shoes on. Test drives and renting give people a chance to experience something before having to commit. A drowning simulator helps people experience how difficult it is to survive without a life jacket. Reducing uncertainty and making people more likely to take action.[14]

Think about the last time you went shopping at the supermarket. What type of fruit did you buy? Or flavor of ice cream?

If you're like most people, you probably bought the same thing you always do. The same type of apples or the same flavor of ice cream. Chocolate, vanilla, or, if you were feeling really bold, maybe mint chocolate chip. Inertia strikes again.

Contrast that with the last time you went to an ice cream parlor. You might not have gotten a completely new flavor, but I bet you picked something more unusual. Something more adventurous. Pistachio, cookies and cream, or maybe even milk chocolate hazelnut.

Are people just more interesting when they eat out? More daring, willing to change, or do something new?

Not really. It's that most ice cream parlors give out samples.

Want to get people to change? Switch from their usual behavior, choice, or action?

Be a catalyst and lower the barrier to trial. Be an ice cream parlor, not a supermarket.

Drive Discovery

Freemium and reducing up-front costs both work if someone is interested in trying something out. But what if people don't even know you exist? Or they know you exist but don't think they'd like what you have to offer?

In 2007, car maker Acura had a problem. It wasn't the product. The cars themselves were pretty good. The MDX had won *Motor Trend*'s sport utility vehicle of the year, and the TSX and RSX had been named to *Car and Driver* magazine's ten best list multiple times.

The issue was consumer perception. Acura made high-quality cars that lasted a long time, but consumers just weren't considering the brand. Acura had been in the United States years before Lexus, but even decades later Lexus had a larger market share. When people thought about buying a Japanese luxury car, Lexus was the brand that came to mind. Acura just wasn't in the consideration set.

Acura thought they could win if they could just get people to try the car. Existing customers loved the brand. They raved about the engine, and when their old car died, they came back in to buy a new one.

There just weren't enough of those people. It was like Acura was an amazing restaurant whose tables sat half-empty because no one knew about it.

Acura was already offering test drives, but this wasn't enough. Test drives helped get interested customers to try the car, but it wasn't solving the awareness and perception problems.

Who takes a test drive? Only people who already know the brand and think they might like it. If people didn't think about Acura or didn't think they'd like driving one, they weren't going to stop by the dealership for a test drive.

When faced with a challenge like this, companies often resort to a standard approach: advertising.

Take Buick. They saw themselves as a premium brand, but the public disagreed. They saw Buick as a boring, fuddy-duddy car that their grandparents drove. So Buick did what many large companies do when they're stuck: they bought a Super Bowl ad.

Buick spent millions on traditional push messaging in an effort to change consumers' minds. It ran campaigns showing graying grandmas saying "Sure doesn't look like a Buick," and they paid Shaquille O'Neal and other celebrities to appear in ads saying how great Buick was.

This failed so miserably that a couple of years later Buick took its brand name off its cars entirely. It decided the only way it could sell Buicks was if consumers weren't reminded that Buick was the brand they were buying.

Acura knew traditional advertising wouldn't solve their problem. Not only was it expensive, but it wouldn't remove the key barrier. Putting butts in seats. Getting people to try Acura.

So, instead of trying to persuade, they brought the car to the people.

Acura partnered with high-end W Hotels to offer an exclusive livery service. Pitched as an extension of the W's Whatever/

Whenever concierge service, anyone staying at any W Hotel could get a ride anywhere in town in an Acura MDX. All guests had to do was book the service and they would be chauffeured across town for free.

You might not have liked Acura. You might have thought it was boring or overpriced, or not even realized the brand existed. But if you were staying at the W and needed a ride somewhere, why not take advantage of the free ride? And along the way, you would learn that the brand was much nicer than you thought.

Which is exactly what over a million people did.

Did all the people who tried the Acura experience buy an Acura? No, of course not. But tens of thousands did. And around 80 percent of them switched from other luxury brands.

Which do you think had greater return on investment? Spending millions trying to convince people that Buick was better than they thought? Or lending the local W Hotel a few cars and giving guests a chance to see how good Acura really is?

The Acura experience changed minds by driving discovery. Because if people don't know something exists, or don't think they'll like it, they're unlikely to go looking to try it.

Acura could have done test drives at W Hotels, but that wouldn't have solved the problem. People who didn't think they'd like an Acura still wouldn't have taken one.

Instead, the company took the "try" out of trial. They delivered the experience a different way, one that didn't demand anything of their potential customers. And in so doing, encouraged a broader set of people to consider the brand.

Supermarkets hand out free samples of smoked sausage on toothpicks. That not only lowers the barrier to trial for sausage lovers, it also grows the set of people who think about buying sausage in the first place.

Trial-size toothpastes in first-class airline amenity kits, or shaving cream samples in hotel bathrooms, serve the same function. Even if someone isn't looking to switch toothpastes, anyone who forgets theirs at home will try the sample, increasing the chance that they will change brands in the future.[15]

Existing customers can also be a valuable opportunity for social trials.

A few years ago I was helping a builder of large apartment buildings grow their brand. We were trying to figure out how to raise awareness and drive more potential customers to come take a tour of the properties, when we hit on a simple solution: Why not encourage residents to have guests over more often?

Giving away party supplies or free catering for big events was an easy way to help more potential residents see inside the units. Following a salesperson around a staged apartment is fine, but who better to share what living there is like than someone who already does?

Kiwi Crate, a subscription box program for educational kids' toys, did something similar. They usually sent subscribers one toy a month, but to encourage growth they started a birthday box program. Parents hosting kids' birthday parties could order a special box that had toys and activities for all the kids to enjoy.

Not only did it keep the kids engaged, this program helped dozens of new people discover the brand. And bring home reminders of how much fun they had. Making it more likely that they become new customers in the future.

Make It Reversible

The last way to reduce uncertainty is to make things reversible.

A few years ago I was thinking about getting a dog. My family always had dogs when I was growing up and I loved being around them. I saw myself as a dog person, jumped at the chance to play with other people's dogs, and would even volunteer at an animal shelter from time to time to get to hang out with dogs more often.

Not surprisingly, then, getting a dog had been on my mind for a while.

But every time I thought about it, the same issues came up: *How do I know which dog to pick? Am I home enough to take care of it? What happens if I'm traveling?*

The barriers were always too high, so I always came away with the conclusion that I wasn't ready to have a dog.

One weekend, though, on the way back to the car after dinner, my girlfriend and I happened to walk by a local animal shelter. Philadelphia's Street Tails Animal Rescue had an eight-week-old puppy in the window, and we had a couple minutes, so we went in to check it out. She was a sweet pit bull mix with an adorable tuxedo coat that ran around in circles and happily gnawed on my fingers as I held her. She seemed wonderful.

But as I thought about adopting her, the same old questions arose: *Will I be home enough? What if she gets too big for where I live?* Etc., etc., etc. I just wasn't sure.

As I set the puppy down and started to walk out of the store, a nice volunteer stopped me. "You seem like you like that puppy," she said.

"Yeah," I replied, "but I'm just not sure I can give her a good home."

"No problem," she said, "but in case it helps, we have a two-week trial period."

A two-week trial?

The shelter wanted to make sure potential adopters were prepared to be pet parents. That the dogs found the right homes. So if for any reason during the first two weeks people felt their home wasn't a good fit, they could bring the dog back.

Suddenly, the barriers to adoption didn't seem so daunting.

My girlfriend and I filled out the paperwork, bought a couple cans of food and a crate, and walked the dog right out of the shelter.

Years later, that girlfriend is my wife, and Zoë is an integral part of our family. And all it took was a two-week trial.

That two-week trial didn't make Zoë any cheaper. We still had to pay for food, shots, a crate, and all the other things a puppy needs.

And it didn't reduce the up-front costs. We still had to purchase all those supplies before we could bring her home.

But it did reduce my uncertainty. Because it *made the decision reversible*. It made me feel that, worst case, if Zoë wasn't happy, we could bring her back without a problem. Which made me more comfortable bringing her home in the first place.

Returns are a big issue for retailers. Consumers return more than a quarter of a trillion dollars in merchandise annually, and less than half of those goods can be resold at full price. In addition to creating problems for inventory management, retailers have to figure out how to restock the sellable goods and triage damaged ones to a string of liquidators and wholesalers.

Not surprisingly, then, many retailers are tightening up their policies. REI and L.L.Bean have replaced their famous lifetime guarantees with stricter limits. Most companies give consumers thirty days to return their purchases, with the expectation that shorter policies will reduce costs and increase profit.

Intuitively, this makes sense. The longer it's been, the harder products become to sell. Clothes go out of fashion and technology gets outdated. So shorter return periods should lead to fewer returns, and the goods that do come back should be in better condition and easier to resell.

But some research suggests this might be shortsighted. Two marketing researchers ran an experiment in which different groups of consumers randomly received different return policies.[16] For the strict policy group, only defective products or incorrect shipments could be returned. For the lenient policy group, any product could be returned at any time for any reason.

Contrary to intuition, the less restrictive policy actually increased profits. Not by just a little, but by 20 percent. Because the lenient policy didn't just increase returns, it also increased sales, and word of mouth. And these increases were more than enough to offset the cost of the extra returned merchandise. Applied to the company's full base of customers, the lenient policy would have increased profits by more than $10 million a year.[17]

Just like reducing up-front costs, shrinking back-end friction encourages action. Like free shipping and free trials, lenient return policies help change minds because they reduce people's hesitation about trying something new. Knowing you can return something anytime helps de-risk the process and makes people more comfortable taking action.

Zappos didn't just offer free shipping; they paired it with free returns. If people didn't like what they ordered, they ended up no worse than when they started.

Money-back guarantees or pay-for-performance contracts work similarly. "Don't like it? We'll fix it." Some lawyers advertise that they don't get paid if the client doesn't win. Even airline tickets are covered by a twenty-four-hour return policy. All of which lower uncertainty and reduce inertia, encouraging customers to change their minds from no to yes.[18]

Taking Advantage of Inertia

For all the ways in which lowering the barrier to trial allows catalysts to overcome uncertainty, one more aspect is worth mentioning.

The mug study we talked about in the Endowment chapter showed that sellers value things more than buyers. That once people have something, they become attached to it and are loath to give it up.

Along these lines, trial takes advantage of the endowment effect by shifting peoples' mind-set from acquisition to retention. Before someone has tried a product, the decision they're considering is acquisition. Whether it's worth the cost or effort to acquire something.

But once someone has already tried that product, they're faced with a different question. Not whether they'd pay $5 to read a magazine but whether they'd pay $5 to *keep reading* it. To not have to give up using it. And while some people may not be willing to pay the market price to acquire something, many more will be willing to pay that price to avoid losing it.

In that way, trial shifts people from potential mug buyers to potential mug sellers. It endows them with the item. Encouraging them to shift from how much they would pay to acquire something to how much they would need to be compensated to give it up. And given that the latter is higher, most people will pay to stay.

Indeed, giving people more time to return things can actually make returns *less* likely.[19] That is, giving people ninety days to return an item rather than thirty days can decrease their likelihood of returning it. People grow attached to the item, they feel greater ownership of it, and it becomes harder to give up.

Actions that encourage trial also cleverly leverage the tendency for inertia. Before a customer orders a pair of shoes, inertia means sticking with the shoes they already have. And given the number of options out there, it's easy to feel choice overload and just do nothing.

But if something like free shipping or returns helps overcome that inertia and leads someone to order a particular pair, the impact of inertia shifts. Now the question isn't whether it is worth the effort to get new shoes but whether it is worth the effort to get rid of the pair that was just ordered.

Once the shoes are already there, it takes effort to box them up, print a return label, and ship them back to the retailer. It takes even more effort to search among the myriad other options that are out there to find a different pair. The shoes themselves are the same, but the alternative just got a lot more effortful. Inertia still rules the day, but in this case, inertia means the new shoes stay put.*

Easier to Try, More Likely to Buy

Neophobia is the fear or a dislike of anything new. In animals, the term is used to describe the tendency to avoid unfamiliar

---

* Trial also subtly shifts decisions from comparisons to single evaluation. When considering what product to buy or service to use, people are often in a comparative mind-set. Which one of the various offerings is better? They compare various options, consider the relative upsides and downsides of each, and pick the one that comes out on top. People maximize, or look for the best thing out there. Once they've tried something, however, that comparative process is often put on hold. Rather than actively searching for the best, they focus on one option and whether that option is good enough. They're satisficing, testing whether this one option is above the bar.

And while they consider that option, they usually abandon the search for alternatives. Instead of continuing to look at other websites, for example, once someone orders shoes to try on, they tend to wait to see if they will work. They're not scanning the horizon for something better; they're focused on the thing in front of them. Making it much more likely they'll end up with it.

Think about being single versus dating one person exclusively. When you're single, you actively search for the best partner. You go on dates with different people, compare them, and consider the relative merits of each. You look for a set of desired attributes, and the list often gets longer the longer you search. This makes it less likely that anyone will ever live up to the growing laundry list, and more likely that you'll never settle down.

When you're dating one person exclusively, however, it's a different set of questions being considered and decisions being made. Rather than always looking for other options or wondering whether you could do better, you're focused on the person you're dating. As long as they are good enough, you keep dating them.

objects or situations, and in children it is often used as part of food neophobia, or an avoidance of new foods.

While most people don't have the clinical version of neophobia, we're all neophobic to some degree. Compared to old things we're already doing, we tend to dislike or undervalue new ones. And part of the reason is uncertainty.

Consequently, encouraging trial is a powerful way to catalyze change. And which strategy to use to do so depends on whose mind needs to be changed and where in their journey or decision-making process they're getting stuck.

If people are interested but not sure, focusing on the front end is often useful. Rather than charging, starting with a free version and, like Dropbox, encouraging people to upgrade to a premium, paid offering. Like Zappos and car dealers, lowering the up-front costs through free shipping, test drives, or similar approaches.

Or, on the back end, like Street Tails Animal Rescue, making things reversible. Using free returns and trial periods to make people feel more comfortable agreeing to change because they know that, worst case, they can change things later.

In cases where people are not aware that something exists, however, or don't think it's a good fit for them, driving discovery helps. Like Acura or Kiwi Crate, bringing things directly to people or using social ties to encourage trial.

All help people un-pause and take action by enabling them to experience something they might not otherwise be willing to try.

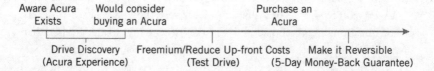

_____

While many examples have focused on getting people to change the products they buy or the services they use, the same principles can be applied to changing things like ideas and life-styles.

Take vegetarianism. Not eating meat is a big switch. Particularly if you love bacon, or a juicy steak, it's tough to go cold turkey.

But things like Meatless Monday provide a low-cost way to test it out. Rather than completely swearing off meat, try skipping it just one day a week and seeing what that feels like. And maybe learning that it's not as hard as one might think.

Trying to get a potential customer or client to buy a new product or service? How can you make it easier for them to try? To get an initial sense of what it would be like without having to invest all the money, time, and energy up-front? To get a taste of what the outcomes or benefits might be like?

Let people experience something in small doses, and if they like it, they'll come back for more.

How to Change the Boss's Mind

To see easing uncertainty in action, it helps to visit a place where even the best new ideas are often stymied by the barriers to change. And that is the office.

The new project seemed doomed. As Jacek Nowak walked out of the meeting, his colleagues' voices kept ringing in his ears. "Why does this matter?" one said. "This is a waste of time," barked another. Even if they did all the work to implement the program, there was no guarantee that customers would care. That clients would actually appreciate the effort they went through. Things were generally going well, so why change?

Jacek had worked in banking for more than a decade. He started in customer service, supporting administrative processes in a bank branch, and worked his way up from there. He had conducted workshops, coordinated training programs, and helped shape recruitment processes. Eventually, rather than training new hires himself, he was responsible for managing a team of trainers. As a branch office manager at Santander Bank, he was responsible for customer service at multiple branches. He managed training and development so that employees would provide the best experience possible.

But some recent mystery shopper research had shown disappointing results. Things were satisfactory—fine, even—but something was missing. Most employees had worked for the company for a while; they knew the products and procedures inside and out. But after repeating the same activities again and again, year after year, the implementation had become mechanical. Staff smiled at customers, just like the handbook suggested, but it was out of obligation rather than any real warmth. Employees stood up when clients came in, as they were supposed to, but briefly and without conviction.

Standards were technically being met or even exceeded, but a closer look revealed troubling patterns. Key performance indicators, like sales of larger loans, insurance, or longer loan periods, were lower than they should have been. Too many people were closing accounts and switching to the competition. Clients were generally satisfied but didn't trust employees enough to talk about their real needs.

Jacek knew that a change was needed. He wanted to improve customer experience. To deepen relationships. To encourage customers to see employees as advisors or helpers rather than as salespeople.

He surveyed best practices from different industries and found that many improvements in customer experience involved some sort of surprise and delight. Surprising people with small gifts and actions made them see that they were recognized and valued. A high-end hotel, for example, greeted customers by name when they walked in and had their favorite beverage waiting in the hotel room.

Jacek thought doing something similar could help the bank. Sending customers cards on their birthdays, greeting them by name, or celebrating their important life milestones. A customer service initiative that would strengthen customers' emotional connection and improve employee morale.

But when he pitched the idea to his boss and other members of senior management, most were opposed. As industries go, banking is extremely traditional. Formally dressed employees sitting behind large wooden desks, much as they did twenty years ago. A focus on interest rates and checking accounts rather than customer experience or employee engagement.

Sending customers handwritten birthday cards? The bank's leadership was skeptical. There's no way this will work, they protested. Branch employees were used to interacting with customers a particular way and they weren't keen on changing. Things were going well enough already, and senior management didn't see the need to mix things up. Any change was seen as a threat.

Jacek tried providing more information. He shared research on customers' feelings and preferences and offered data suggesting that price was not the most important thing when people make decisions. He even had an outside consultant specializing in customer experience come in to talk about the latest tools and approaches.

But still people objected. Things are different in banking, his boss said. Customers care about quick, efficient service, not building relationships. Sales are sales. This might work in some industries but not here. Not with us.

This response is something people often get from their bosses. No, thanks. Maybe later. That's great for a different organization, but it won't work here.

It's almost as if bosses come preprogrammed to say no. Not only are they busy, but they usually have a clear agenda set out before them, and they're not interested in deviating. They see their path to promotion as doing things as they've always been done, so anything that diverges from that is seen as an unnecessary risk.

Jacek needed a way to get people to come around. A way to convince management, and employees, that this new initiative would actually work. A way to reduce their uncertainty about this new initiative he was proposing.

But the more Jacek tried to persuade people, the more pushback he got. The more opposed to the project they became.

Frustrated and discouraged, Jacek tried one last approach. Working with a small team, he got to know more about each branch employee and their life, even his boss and the other members of the senior management team. Birthdays and wedding anniversaries, but also more unusual things like their dream holidays and when they started working at the company. Positive things like their favorite foods, but also more challenging things like family illnesses and other things they were struggling with.

Then, using this information, he created a unique experience to surprise and move each person. For a branch manager's birthday, they organized a treasure hunt throughout the city, creating various activities at different sights and locations. Two people going on a difficult hiking trip were sent warm hats. A senior leader was sent a handwritten note celebrating her ten-year service with the company and noting, "You have been with us for 3,650 days, which gives a minimum of 5,256,000 of your genius smiles, without which our work would not be half as pleasant. Thank you."

Others received special gifts, gadgets, or caring expressions of support. Always personal, always tailored, and often highly emotional.

One employee's son had been in a car accident, so Jacek's team founded a Facebook group and took up a collection for treatment. In a few hours it had thousands of members, and soon they had the necessary sum to pay the hospital.

Anyone would be happy with a huge television. That would be easy. But to write a few words, personally and accurately, was what generated the most emotion.

Recipients were stunned. All were surprised and many were deeply moved. Touched that someone had taken the time to care.

A few weeks later, Jacek began the normal senior leadership meeting with a question: "How did you feel when you received that thoughtful, compassionate expression of caring?"

The answers were clear. The gestures had made a huge impression on everyone.

Now Jacek's team could talk about the importance of emotion, outline the new initiative, and discuss the value of customer experience. All without fear that someone would say it wouldn't work. Because it had already worked for everyone in the room.

Years later, the initiative lives on. Employees not only celebrate client birthdays and weddings but they approach customer interactions with empathy. They are committed to discovering each client's unique, individual needs and eager to look for unusual solutions.

Things went so well, the board of the bank started a new customer experience management team and appointed Jacek as its manager.

More importantly, though, Jacek had taken a project that seemed on the brink of failure and turned it around. He not only got his boss to believe in something the boss was initially against but got him to embrace it wholeheartedly.

Rather than trying to convince senior management how important customer experience is, Jacek eased their uncertainty. Not by pushing or providing more facts and figures, but by being a catalyst and enabling management to experience it themselves. By lowering the barrier to trial and helping senior management try out what he was suggesting.

And through these efforts, Jacek did something that often seems impossible. He changed the boss's mind.

So far, we've discussed how to reduce reactance, ease endowment, shrink distance, and alleviate uncertainty. Next we examine the last barrier catalysts frequently face. And that is situations where there is not enough evidence.

5. Corroborating Evidence

Growing up, Phil never thought he would start a drug and alcohol counseling company. He also never thought he would be a heroin addict.

Phil appeared to have a pretty good life. He had earned a bachelor's degree in finance, and started working for a Fortune 500 telecommunications company in the Midwest. He excelled at work, moved to a Big Five accounting firm, and became what seemed like a model employee.

Underneath it all, though, Phil was the poster child of a functioning addict. When Phil was nineteen, a friend had given him a couple Vicodin. He liked the way it felt and started taking more. Borrowing extras from friends, filling fake prescriptions, even ransacking people's medicine cabinets looking for pills.

Phil thought he could stop. He made a deal with himself that if he got into college to study business, he would quit. He got in and he quit, cold turkey. He stopped using, proving to himself there was no problem. He was in control.

Everything was fine until a few years later, when someone gave Phil some pills as a graduation gift and he made the choice to take them.

At first he only took them once in a while. But soon his habit escalated to dangerous levels. Phil was using every day and doing everything he could to cover it up. Filling fake prescriptions again while telling everyone things were fine.

Phil's family knew but didn't really think of him as an addict. To them, an addict was someone who didn't have a job and stole to support their habit. As long as Phil had a job, they thought he'd eventually come around. If he only met the right girl to take care of him, he'd stop.

Instead, Phil got arrested on a felony fake prescription charge. He lost his job and moved back home. Then he graduated to heroin.

Once that happened, Phil's life spiraled out of control pretty quickly. More arrests followed, and he spent ninety days in jail. He started stealing to pay for his habit. Taking money from friends and family or stealing things and hocking them at a local pawnshop.

His family tried to get Phil to change. His dad yelled; his mom cried. They begged and pleaded and threatened to kick him out. They sent him to one nearby treatment program after another. Various state-funded programs. Nineteen in total. And none worked.

Phil would always find a way to convince his family to take him back. To make them believe that this time would be different. He even convinced his parents to let him sign a contract promising that he would turn over a new leaf. All it did was teach him to become a better liar.

Phil's family did everything they could think of. They even

waited for him to hit rock bottom. But regardless of what they tried, Phil wouldn't stop using. He still thought he was in control.

Pebbles and Boulders

To understand how substance abuse counselors get addicts to change, we need to start outside the realm of drugs and alcohol. To learn about the distinction behavioral scientists make between weak and strong attitudes.

How much do you like the word "juvalamu"? What about "chakaka"?

You might like "juvalamu" more (most people do) or prefer "chakaka," but more importantly you probably don't care that much about either.

Opinions toward these nonsense words are examples of what are called weak attitudes. Preferences or opinions that people don't find very important, that haven't received much thought, or that are relatively easy to change.

If I told you that Juvalamu was the name of a dictator who murdered his political enemies, you probably wouldn't like that word anymore. That one piece of information would be enough to change your view.

How do you feel about pine trees? Prime numbers? Serif versus sans serif fonts? For most people, these are examples of weakly held attitudes. You have an opinion, but it's not that important to you and it's relatively easy to change.

Contrast that with how you feel about different political parties or your favorite sports team. How you feel about your favorite brand of beer. Or abortion.

These are examples of strong attitudes. High-involvement issues, topics, or preferences that you've thought a lot about or hold with great moral conviction. Things you feel aren't just a matter of opinion but have a right or wrong answer.

Not surprisingly, strong attitudes are much more resistant to change.

Imagine that an article suggests your favorite celebrity said something racist. What's your first reaction? It's probably one of disbelief or denial. There's no way that person could be racist.

Unlike hearing that Juvalamu was a dictator, our anti-persuasion radar rushes to protect our strong beliefs. Rather than giving up or changing our mind, we discount information that goes against our existing views, picking it apart rather than revising our perspective.

Just like a really bad headache needs stronger medicine, some issues, products, and behaviors need more before people will change. More proof or evidence is required.

If a good friend recommends a new website, that one endorsement is probably enough to encourage you to take a look. You trust your friend's opinion, and it's not that effortful to check out, so their recommendation drives action.

But say they just put solar panels on their house. Or that they joined a movement against income inequality, tried a risky medical procedure, or started ordering all their groceries online. Would that be enough for you to do the same?

Probably not.

The same holds for organizations considering an employee training program or leaders considering a new management strategy. Hearing that another organization is doing the same thing may be helpful but is probably not enough to drive action.

For strong attitudes, there is a higher threshold for changing minds. More is needed. More information, more texture, or more certainty. More proof before people will switch.

Changing minds, then, is a bit like trying to lift something on the other end of a seesaw.

How much weight, or proof, you need depends on how heavy the thing is that you're trying to move. If you're trying to lift a pebble, you don't need much. Add a little evidence and it moves right away. Change happens.

But if you're trying to move a boulder, much more effort is needed. More proof is required before people will change.

The Translation Problem

When faced with a boulder, the most common response is to turn up the juice. To try harder to convince people that a certain course of action is the right way to go. As the proverb says: If at first you don't succeed, try, try again.

Spouse not interested in the more expensive vacation package? Try a different appeal. Client still wavering on whether to make an order? Call again in a week.

And indeed, following up works. Sometimes.

Advertising research finds that multiple exposures can encourage action.[1] Consumers may not pay attention the first time, so seeing an ad a second, third, or even fourth time gives them more opportunities to gather information and consider different aspects of an issue or proposal.

But as anyone who has left the room when a TV commercial came on for the umpteenth time can attest, there are downsides to multiple exposure. Hearing the same pitch again and again gets boring, tedious, and irritating. Listeners know what's going to happen, so they tune it out or turn it off.

Would-be persuaders often try to solve this problem through variation. One commercial presents one feature and a different commercial presents another. Salespeople focus on one benefit the first time they call and mention another the second time around.

Unfortunately, this usually fails. Salespeople think they're providing "more context" or "sweetening the deal," but to listeners it's just another flavor of the same pitch. Another persuasion attempt to react against. If they weren't convinced the first time, now they're even less likely to listen.

But there's another reason trying again doesn't work. A far subtler one. And that is the translation problem.

Imagine someone comes into the office Monday morning and tells you that they watched an amazing show over the weekend. The dialogue is sharp, the plot is gripping, and the acting is superb. They just loved it and they think you'll like it too.

They've just added some weight to the other end of the seesaw. And depending on your threshold for change or how strongly you feel about television shows, that amount of evidence either is or is not enough to encourage action. If your preferences are more like a pebble, a little proof is enough and things change. You'll watch the show. If your preferences are more like a boulder, you'll consider the recommendation, but that won't be enough to get you to watch it. Nothing changes.

Now Thursday rolls around, they've watched another episode, and they continue to be enthusiastic. "The second episode is just as good!" they exclaim. "I can't wait to see what's going to happen next!"

Their enthusiasm isn't meaningless. After all, the second episode could have bombed. Showrunners usually use the first episode to sell the show to a network, so it's often their best work. Great pilots don't always translate into great shows, so knowing your coworker liked another episode is certainly encouraging.

That said, knowing they liked the second episode doesn't add that much additional information. You already know they liked the show. So the fact that they liked the second episode as well isn't that surprising. It doesn't add much more evidence. If their first endorsement didn't drive you to action, the second one probably isn't going to, either.

Because when someone endorses or recommends something, there's always a translation problem. A puzzle.

When your coworker says a show is great, that could mean the show is really, truly great. But it might also just reflect the fact that they like lots of shows. Or that they like all sitcoms or anything with a strong female lead.

When someone hears a recommendation, they try to make sense of it. To sort out what that recommendation means. Does it say something about the *thing* being recommended, or does it just say something about the *recommender* themselves?

But even if the recommender doesn't recommend many shows, another question arises: Sure, *they* liked the show, but does that mean *I'll* like it?

Because impact depends on more than just credibility. There's also an issue of fit. Yes, someone may have lots of expertise in a certain domain, but preferences are heterogeneous. Some people like sitcoms and other people hate them. Some people love romantic comedies and others can't stand them.

So whenever people get a recommendation or see someone else doing or liking something, they try to figure out—to translate—what it means for them. How informative is that person's opinion? What does it say about their own likely reaction?

If the coworker who recommended the show was another you, there would be less of an issue. Not just an identical twin but literally Another You. Someone who has the same preferences, likes, and dislikes. Someone who has the same needs, concerns, and values.

Another You liked the show? You'll probably like it as well. Another You installed solar panels on their house and is happy with the choice? You'll probably be happy with it as well. Because if Another You liked the show or found solar panels worth installing, it's pretty certain you'll feel the same.

But in the absence of this perfect doppelgänger, people have to make inferences. How much does the fact that someone else likes something indicate about how much I'll like it? How predictive is the fact something worked for their organization about whether it will work for me and mine?

This translation problem doesn't happen for everything. Someone tells you the final score of the game or who won the election? There's no need for translating. If someone shares that information, who they are or what they like is irrelevant. The final score is the final score is the final score. The election winner is the election winner. It's factual. It's objective.

But when it comes to changing minds, translation comes into play. Not everyone likes or believes the same thing. And what works for one person or organization doesn't necessarily work for another. Things are subjective rather than objective.

So how do we solve the translation problem?

Fighting Substance Abuse

Memorial Day morning, 2005. Phil got up, rolled out of bed, and left the house to get high.

When he got home around noon, covered in an oily heroin sheen, his mother, father, and entire family were sitting in the living room. His brother, his sisters, and even some of his neighbors were there. Everyone who was close to Phil. Twelve people in all.

And with them were two strangers Phil didn't recognize. One was an intervention counselor.

Phil felt angry and betrayed. He even considered storming out of the house.

But then his family started talking. They had written letters telling him how much they loved him and cared about him, but how his actions were hurting everyone.

And when they read the letters it was tough not to listen. Each was heartfelt and powerful. They talked about how much they loved Phil. How sad they were. How much they missed him and wanted him back.

Family was everything to Phil. And he could see that he was tearing his to shreds. His mom and dad were at odds, and his brother didn't want to come to the house when Phil was there.

If you want to be a drug addict or an alcoholic, we can't stop you, they said. But if you want to get high, you're not going to do it here. Not anymore.

Phil was a big guy. His parents were worried that he would beat the crap out of everyone. There's no way he'll go back to rehab, said Phil's mother. He's the most stubborn person you've ever met. The interventionist heard more excuses from Phil's mom than he heard from fifty addicts in a month.

Phil didn't have to seek treatment. He could have kept doing dope, stealing, and doing all the horrible things that come with addiction. He didn't have to go to rehab.

But seeing all those people together had an impact. Hearing

how they all felt the same way changed something. It forced Phil to take note. To realize how much his behavior had impacted the people around him. To realize how it had hurt his family. To realize he was an addict.

His mom had tried to get him to change hundreds of times, but this time was different. Phil broke down and accepted help.

Interventionists are often the last line of defense. They get only the toughest cases. By the time an addict gets to them, all other options have usually been exhausted. Because if it was easy to change that person's mind, he or she wouldn't be there. Someone else would have gotten them to quit already. The fact that a person is speaking with an interventionist indicates that others have tried and failed. That people have asked, begged, yelled, screamed, and threatened. All to no avail.

Interventions are no cure-all. To get addicts to change, their entire ecosystem has to be altered. Without realizing it, friends and family members may be unintentionally enabling the problem. So for change to stick, the whole system has to change as well.[2]

But in the right circumstances, as part of a broader solution, interventions can be a helpful first step on the journey to wellness. Because interventions solve the translation problem. They help address a particular sticking point: people don't believe they have a problem.

Nearly half of Americans have a close friend or family member who's been addicted to drugs. And most addicts are in denial. They don't believe they need to change.

Part of the challenge is that an alcoholic or a drug addict may not remember. If someone says, "Dave, you have a problem. Last night you yelled at me or wrapped your car around a lamppost," Dave may say he doesn't know. Not because he's trying to be malicious, but because he blacked out. He has no memory of what he did.

But it's more than that.

Because even if Dave remembers what happens, there's the challenge of belief. Dr. Vernon E. Johnson, one of the forefathers of interventions, notes that "rationalization and projection work together to block the chemically dependent person's awareness of the disease. By keeping the alcoholic or drug addict out of touch with reality, they eventually make it impossible for him or her to understand that a problem exists."[3]

Put another way, most addicts don't think they have an issue, otherwise they would have done something about it already. And if an addict doesn't believe they have a problem, is one person really going to change their mind?

It's easy to discount one person's perspective. Make them the crazy one. Sure, you might think I have a drinking problem, but you're only one person, so that might just be your opinion. And when there is one of you and one of me, who am I going to trust? That's easy. Me.

But it's harder to discount a chorus. If multiple people are saying the same thing at the same time, it's harder to ignore.

A group carries the necessary weight to break through. If a bunch of friends and family members are all sitting there saying there's a problem, it's harder to think they're all biased and misguided. Even though the addict might disagree, the fact that they're all consistent makes it harder not to at least consider what they are saying.

And harder not to go seek treatment as a result.[4]

Strength in Numbers

From drug abuse and eating disorders to addictive gambling and alcoholism, interventions help people face the fact that they have a problem. They help break the web of denial and get addicts to consider that their behavior might be having negative consequences.

Even beyond substance abuse, though, there's strength in numbers. Corporate boards wait to adopt new practices until they've been adopted by several peer institutions. Doctors wait to adopt new drugs until they see multiple colleagues using them. And companies wait to adopt supply chain technologies and management strategies until they've been piloted by a number of other firms.[5]

Multiple sources saying or doing the same thing solves the translation problem. If just one source suggests or does something, it's hard to translate. Hard to know if their opinion is diagnostic. Hard to know what their reaction means for your own.

But if multiple sources say or do something, it's harder not to listen. Because now there's corroborating evidence. Reinforcement. Multiple sources concur. They have the same view, response, or preference. And this consistency means it's much more likely that you'll feel the same way.

One other doctor prescribing a new treatment? Maybe a sales rep came by or they have a certain type of patient. But multiple colleagues prescribing the same thing? Might be worth taking a deeper look.

If multiple people are doing the same thing, it's harder to argue that they're wrong. Harder to argue that the thing they're suggesting or recommending isn't any good.

Multiple sources also add credibility and legitimacy. Increasing the expectation that others will approve and lowering the risk of embarrassment or sanction.

One person might have quirky tastes, but two people? Five people? Ten people? The more sources speaking in concert, the more corroborating evidence it provides. The less likely it says something about the sources themselves rather than the quality of what they're doing or recommending. And the more likely you'll like it as well.[6]

As the old adage goes, "If one person says you have a tail, you laugh and think they're crazy. But if three people say it, you turn around to look."

More sources doing or saying the same thing can provide more proof. But who those sources are and when they share their perspectives plays an important role.

In particular, when finding corroborating evidence, it's important to consider who, when, and how: (1) *who* else to involve (or which sources are most impactful), (2) *when* to space corroborating evidence over time, and (3) *how* to best deploy scarce resources when trying to change minds on a larger scale.

Which Sources Are Most Impactful?

Corroborating evidence helps change minds by providing social reinforcement. But who is most useful in that process? Are all sources weighted equally, or do certain ones provide more proof?

In late 2001, students from La Trobe University in Melbourne, Australia, were recruited for a study on how people respond to audio presentations.[7] The students were directed to show up at a laboratory, and when they arrived, they sat down at a desk and put on a pair of headphones. They were told they would listen to a series of audiotapes and make judgments about them.

The experimenters behind the study were interested in what makes people laugh. And in particular how laughter is shaped by social influence.

They had participants listen to what sounded like a live recording of a stand-up comedian, and for some listeners the tape included canned laughter. What people find funny might seem totally subjective, but hearing prerecorded merriment helps prime the pump. (Indeed, traditional sitcoms like *Seinfeld* and *Friends* often used so-called laugh tracks to get both the live audience and viewers at home to join in.)

As expected, the laugh track helped. By discreetly observing participants from behind a two-way mirror, scientists found that listeners were more likely to laugh and smile at the comedian's jokes when they heard other people laughing.

But beyond the mere presence of laughter, the scientists also manipulated *who* listeners thought was laughing.

One group of listeners was told that the laughers were people like them, or other La Trobe University students.

Another group of listeners were told that the laughers were different: members of a political party with whom the students did not identify.

Even though the laughter sounded exactly the same, whoever the listeners thought was laughing shaped their reaction. When listeners thought the laughers were not like them, the fact that those people were laughing didn't matter. It didn't change their behavior. Listeners laughed the same amount as when there was no laugh track at all.

But when listeners thought the laughers were people like them, they changed their behavior. They laughed nearly four times as long.

A great deal of research finds that similarity matters.[8] Someone like me thinks a joke is funny? I'll probably find it funny as well. But if someone who is not like me finds it funny, that doesn't provide as much information about my likely reaction. Because the more similar a source is, the more diagnostic their experiences, preferences, and opinions are as a source of information.

Looking at hotels on TripAdvisor? You don't just want to know whether a hotel is highly rated; you want to know if that hotel is highly rated among people *like you*. If you're a family traveling with two kids, you probably want a place that other families recommend. The fact that hip twenty-two-year-olds like the hotel isn't as useful.

In fact, if hip twenty-two-year-olds seem to like the hotel, you may even want to avoid it completely. And if you're a hip twenty-two-year-old, you probably feel the same way about families.

In other words, the translation problem is less of a problem when there's less need for translation. In the absence of Another You, similar sources are the next closest thing. Sources that are dealing with the same issues or challenges. Other people with the same needs. Other companies in the same vertical. The more similar they are, the more proof or corroborating evidence they provide, and the greater their impact.

If you're Ashton, a recent college grad dealing with alcohol abuse, it's easy to think you're not an alcoholic. Because in your mind an "alcoholic" doesn't look anything like you. An "alcoholic" is someone who lost everything because of drinking. An "alcoholic" is homeless, can't keep a job, and doesn't have any friends.

And your life might not look anything like that. You might have a loving family, lots of great friends, and a promising future. You're not what you think of as an "alcoholic"—even if you recently got a DUI, black out regularly, or get irritable when you're not drinking. Who doesn't?

So you think recovery groups like Alcoholics Anonymous will be a waste of time because they don't apply to you. Because the people you imagine being there aren't like you at all.

And if you happen to stop by one meeting just to appease your parents, your first impression might be that you're right. One guy looks homeless and that person has the shakes. *They're nothing like me,* you think. *I don't have the problem they have.*

But wait: that guy's a physician? What's he doing here? That guy's a judge? Holy crap. You start seeing people who are "successful." People who have advanced degrees and high-paying jobs. People who have gotten places you want to be. People who are similar.

And when you see people like you—or people you aspire to be like—have problems with alcohol, it makes it harder not to listen to what they're saying. And harder not to change as a result.

Beyond similarity, however, another factor is at play.

Recently a researcher from the Netherlands investigated how social ties influence political donations.[9] Donations are a vital part of the political process. Candidates need money to run advertisements, pay staffers, and even arrange transportation from place to place. But raising such donations can be hard. People are busy and wary about supporting a candidate who might lose in the end. What might motivate more people to give?

Looking at more than 50,000 potential donors, the Dutch researcher examined how a person's likelihood of donating depended on whether their social connections had donated. Whether someone was more likely to give money to a presidential candidate if their friends, family members, or colleagues had given money as well.

Not surprisingly, donations were shaped by social influence. People were more likely to donate if they knew someone else who had already donated.

Further, consistent with the value of corroborating evidence, the number of those connections also mattered. The more prior donors someone knew, the more likely they were to donate. Knowing two donors made donation more likely than knowing just one, and additional donors increased donation even further.

But beyond just the *number* of donors, the type of connection between those donors also played a role.

Imagine you're thinking of donating and you find out that two of your friends have already donated. Which would make you more likely to donate: if those friends knew each other and were part of the same social group, or if they didn't know each other and were completely independent?

Similarity matters for changing minds, as we know, but it turns out diversity is also important. People were more likely to donate when the prior donors they knew came from separate, independent groups. If one was a family member and another was a coworker, people were more than twice as likely to donate. But if they were two family members or two coworkers, multiple sources didn't have as much impact.[10]

Because it's not just about how *many* others are doing something; it's about whether those others provide *additional information*.

More sources doing or supporting something can provide corroborating evidence, but repeated signals from the same group can be redundant. If two people who both like comedies say a show is good, it's still easy to write it off as hitting only a certain group. Same with two people who are good friends. You assume one person already told the other, so the second recommendation doesn't add much.

But if they have differing tastes, or come from different areas of your life, the second source provides more proof.

In fact, if multiple sources are too redundant, they're often grouped together and treated as just a single source. If two people from Accounting recommend the same supplier, for example, people may cluster them into one "Accounting recommendation" rather than treating them as separate pieces of evidence.

The more independent the sources are, the more corroborating evidence they provide.

On the surface, similarity and diversity may seem contradictory. After all, in some ways, the two aspects seem like opposites. If multiple sources are all similar to a target individual or organization, it seems like they would be less diverse.

But that's not necessarily the case.

Take your friends. Each is probably similar to you on some dimensions, but those dimensions are not necessarily the same. One friend may share the same taste in music, while another leans the same way politically. Both are similar to you but in different ways.

The same goes for organizations. Some peers may be the same

size, while others are in the same industry. Both are similar but for different reasons.

Consequently, similarity and diversity can work in concert.

Rather than trying to push prospects, smart companies often let their existing clients do the talking. They host events, such as dinners, where, in addition to hearing from thought leaders or sitting through demos, potential clients can interact with current ones to get an outside perspective. An unbiased view of what working with the company is really like.

But when thinking about where to seat a prospect at dinner, or how best to change their mind, it's important to mix similarity and diversity. Seat them between an existing client in the same industry and another one who's in a different industry but of similar size. Encourage them to talk to one existing client with similar technical needs and another based in the same region.

Sources that are similar enough to the target but different enough from one another offer the perfect combination. Similarity makes the feedback seem diagnostic and relevant. Independence increases the chance that each adds additional value rather than being seen as redundant.

The Science of When

The right mix of sources can provide more proof, but it's also important to understand *when* exposure to these sources will have the most impact.

Interventions are a powerful tool to help addicts change. To seek treatment and get clean. But their value brings up an interesting question.

In most cases, it's not the first time the people in the room have spoken to the addict about their addiction. At different points, different friends and family members have noted their concerns, made requests, or demanded action. They may say something new at the intervention itself, but it's not like the addict doesn't know their point of view.

So if the addict has already been exposed to these multiple sources, why haven't they changed already? That is to say, what's different about the intervention that makes it more effective?

One possibility is the interventionist. Intervention counselors are trained to structure interventions to maximize effectiveness. They're experts at creating a plan, forming the right team, and shaping the written statements that friends and family often create.

Another possibility is the way the sentiments are expressed. While past interactions might have been abstract, angry, and confrontational, interventionists encourage participants to present reality in a receivable way. Rather than yelling or trying to punish the addict, speaking nonjudgmentally, with love and compassion, showing them how much others care.

Both these features are certainly important. But there's a third aspect that also deserves note. Rather than being dripped out in conversations over months, or even years, the intervention compresses everything. It concentrates multiple sources at the same time. All at once rather than over an extended period.

A few years ago my colleague Raghu Iyengar and I analyzed user growth of a new website.[11] Like many new sites, this website didn't have much money to spend on advertising, so they used existing users to help spread the word. Each user could send out invitations through Facebook, and we analyzed how those invitations influenced whether potential new users joined the site.

Consistent with the value of corroborating evidence, people who got more invitations were more likely to join. Compared to someone who got only one invitation, for example, potential users who got a second invite were almost twice as likely to sign up.

But beyond how *many* invitations people received, *when* they received those invitations also mattered. The closer the different invitations were in time, the bigger their collective impact.

To understand why, it helps to go back to the coworker recommending a show. If they tell you how much they love it, and another coworker says something similar the next day, it's hard not to at least consider checking out the show. It's a hot topic, lots of people are talking about it, so you infer that the show must be pretty good.

Spread those conversations out a bit more, though, and their effect is muted.

If one coworker says something today, and another mentions the show three weeks from now, it's less likely to drive action. It's been a while since you heard about the show, so you're less likely to infer it's widely popular. You've probably heard about a lot of other shows in the meantime. And if enough time passes, you may not even remember hearing about the show in the first place.

Addiction researchers note that even when multiple friends and family members try to get an addict to change, their efforts are usually spread out. After noticing some erratic behavior, a friend may make an offhand comment. Two months later a different friend may say something else. It's not until something more serious happens, like an accident or arrest, that a more direct conversation occurs.

But the separation between these expressions weakens their collective impact. If two people say different things at different times, it's easier to shrug them off as unrelated incidents, or come up with alternate attributions. Forget they happened or discount the last interaction by the time the next one occurs.

Our analysis of user growth found something similar. Each invitation provided some evidence that the website was good or worth joining. Over time, though, it was like some of that proof disappeared or evaporated. Like water steaming off a hot road, the more time that elapsed until the second invitation, the less proof that was left from the first one. After one month, the invitation provided only 20 percent as much impact as it had initially. After two months, it had almost no impact at all. As though people had never even received it.*

But concentration mitigated the decline. Just like hearing the same thing from multiple family members at once encourages action, we found that receiving multiple website invitations within a shorter period catalyzed change.

Take two people, one who got two invitations in quick succession and one who received them a month or two apart. The person who received the two invitations one right after the other was over 50 percent more likely to join the site.

---

* In other words, the impact of an invitation diminished quickly, losing 80 percent of its value each month. An invitation one month provided only 20 percent as much impact the next month, and only 4 percent the following month.

When trying to change minds, then, not all proof is equal. Concentrating proof boosts its effectiveness.

Trying to increase attention for a new service or important social cause? Make sure that different media hits happen soon after one another so potential supporters hear about it multiple times in a short period.

Indeed, another study we ran found that exposing people to multiple articles in rapid succession about a pressing social issue, such as sexual assault, increased action. It led more people to sign a petition to help sexual assault survivors and increased donations to the cause. Rather than spreading those same articles out, concentrating them in time boosted support.

Trying to change the boss's mind? After stopping by her office, catalysts encourage colleagues to make a similar suggestion right away. Concentration increases impact.[12]

When to Concentrate or Spread Out Scarce Resources

Concentration is helpful when trying to change one person's mind, but it also has implications for larger-scale change. When trying to transform an organization, spark a social movement, or get a product, service, or idea to catch on.

Take a new home goods start-up that's trying to gain traction. Resources, whether time, money, or personnel, are often limited, so there's a tradeoff between breadth and depth. There are only enough marketing dollars to spend, so choices have to be made.

Spread resources out and run ads in ten different markets, going after a small number of potential customers in each? Or concentrate resources and go after a larger number of potential customers in one market, using that beachhead to grow to nearby markets?

The same holds for getting a social movement to take off. There are not usually enough resources to hold rallies or events in every city right away, so tradeoffs must be weighed. Concentrate on one city and hold multiple events there, or spread efforts out across different cities, holding just a single event in each one?

These two approaches can be described as sprinkler and fire hose strategies.

Sprinklers spread water out. They sprinkle a little here and a little there, providing broad coverage relatively quickly. That coverage isn't deep in any one place, but many places get attention. All the grass within range gets a little wet.

Fire hoses are more concentrated. Rather than spreading water out, they saturate one area. Consequently, hitting multiple areas happens sequentially rather than simultaneously. Drenching one area first and only then moving on to another.

Conventional wisdom says that the sprinkler strategy is better. It raises broader awarencss, diversifies risk, and increases the chance of a first-mover advantage.

If the home goods start-up eventually wants to build a customer base in ten markets, it seems better to spread resources out. After all, concentrating just in New York City to start means it's going to take a while before things spill over to Boston or DC, and even longer to make it out to Los Angeles. Friends and social ties tend to be local, so even if word of mouth helps carry the message, it will take some time to jump from one market to the next.

But is conventional wisdom right? Is a sprinkler strategy always more effective?

It depends. And what it depends on is whether the thing you're trying to change is a weak attitude or a strong one. A pebble or a boulder.

Take two different cities, New York and Los Angeles, and, for simplicity's sake, imagine each has only four people. New York City has persons A, B, C, and D, and Los Angeles has persons E, F, G, and H. In real life, people tend to be more connected to others who are geographically close, so assume something similar here. People are densely connected within cities but not between them. And people share things with their friends, so if one person knows about something, they'll tell the others.

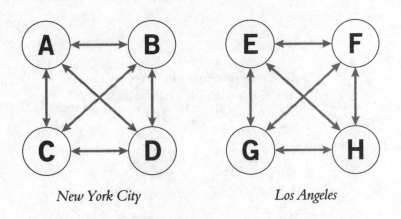

New York City   *Los Angeles*

If there are only enough resources to target two people, which is better? Spreading things out and targeting one person in each market? Or concentrating resources and going after two people in the same place?

For weaker attitudes, pebbles—or cases where only a little proof is needed to generate change—the sprinkler strategy works best. People spread the word to their friends, so reaching one person in each market means eventually reaching all of them. Reach person A in New York, for example, and they'll tell persons B, C, and D. Reach person E in Los Angeles and they'll tell everyone else.

And if just a little proof is enough to change minds, hearing from just person A will be enough to get each of them to change. It makes sense to spread things out and target one person in each market.

In fact, concentration would waste resources. People would hear about something more times than they would need to for change to occur, and the resources could have been better spent elsewhere.

Eventually the fire hose soaks things so completely that there's no need for more, and the water just runs off.

**Effectiveness of Sprinkler Approach
for Weak Attitudes ("Pebbles")**

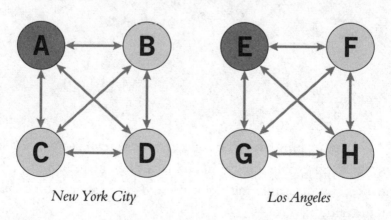

New York City   *Los Angeles*

Total adopters = 8

But what if people need corroborating evidence? What if they need to hear from multiple sources before they'll change?

For stronger attitudes, "boulders," or cases where more proof is needed, the sprinkler strategy won't garner as much traction. Reach person A in New York and they'll still tell B, C, and D. But because people need to hear from multiple sources before they'll change, hearing from just person A won't be enough. Target just one person in each market and they'll tell everyone they know, but no one else will change.

**Effectiveness of Sprinkler Approach
for Strong Attitudes ("Boulders")**

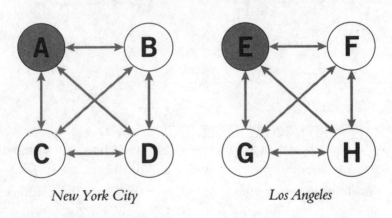

New York City   Los Angeles

Total adopters = 2

Consequently, when more corroborating evidence is needed, using a fire hose is more effective. Rather than targeting one person in two markets (i.e., person A and person E), concentrate all the efforts in one place (i.e., person A and person B). Both recipients will tell their friends, and because each prospect has heard from two others, they'll change as well. It will take more time to eventually reach the second market, but the fire hose will provide enough proof for people to change.

Effectiveness of Fire Hose Approach for Strong Attitudes ("Boulders")

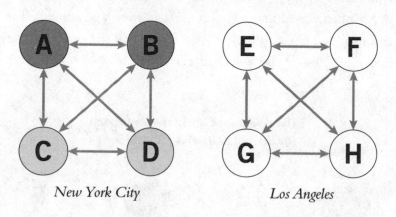

New York City   Los Angeles

Total adopters = 4

The same idea applies within regions.

Individuals and organizations can be classified into different segments: groups or types of people and businesses.

And just like geographic regions, social ties tend to be stronger within groups than between them. Teenagers tend to be friends with other teens, and moms tend to hang out with other moms. The accounting department folks talk to each other more than they talk to the marketing team, and human resources representatives spend more time with each other than they do with IT.

Whether it's better to concentrate resources in one group or spread them out across two or more groups depends on the threshold for change.

If a little proof is enough to drive action, then a sprinkler strategy is ideal. Go after each group simultaneously without much depth.

But when corroborating evidence is needed, concentrating resources becomes more important. Focus on teens first and later go after moms. Target just the Accounting group initially, then move on to Marketing. Create social incubators where people can't help but hear from multiple sources, increasing the likelihood that they'll switch too.

Pebble or Boulder?

When trying to change minds, it's important to be able to judge the difference between pebbles and boulders. Between attitudes and opinions, products and services, behaviors, ideas, and initiatives that need only a little proof versus ones that need a lot more.

Political views, for example, are more difficult to change than font preferences (at least for most people). What type of software a company uses is tougher to shift than what type of paper they buy. Even among something like brand preferences, how fixed they are depends on the category. Preferences for soda are stronger than those for dish soap. Attitudes toward car brands are stronger than those toward paper towels.

To get a sense of whether something is more like a pebble or a boulder, think about how easy it is to change. The more expensive, time-consuming, risky, or controversial something is, the less likely it is to be a pebble and the more likely it is to be a boulder. Something that requires more proof.

Take monetary costs. A $9 stapler shouldn't be too difficult to get people to purchase. A colleague's recommendation or a post on a blog is probably sufficient. But a $9 million digital transformation? A lot more proof is needed.

The same goes for risk. Encouraging someone to try Lasik, a laser vision correction procedure that has been done millions of times, requires some work. The risk isn't nonexistent, but it's a proven procedure. Getting that same person to try a new, less tested procedure? Much more evidence is needed to make them feel comfortable enough to give it a try.

The more that is at stake, the greater the financial cost, and the higher the reputational risk, the more proof or evidence that is needed.

Moving boulders is tough but not impossible. Like interventionists, we need to solve the translation problem by finding corroborating evidence. The more proof that is needed, the more important multiple sources become. We need to find similar but diverse others who provide consistent perspectives, and concentrate those sources in time so their benefit doesn't evaporate. And when trying to achieve larger scale change, we need to think about whether to concentrate or spread out scarce resources. The bigger the boulder, the more a fire hose is better than a sprinkler.

Since he got clean, Phil has dedicated his life to serving others. He became an intervention counselor himself, helping hundreds of people reclaim their lives from drug and alcohol abuse.

Because stopping substance abuse isn't usually something people can do alone. They need reinforcement. As Phil notes:

A lot of people that you deal with, they're college graduates, they're accomplished, they're such great people. I mean, addicts and alcoholics are extremely loving, caring, brilliant people. And families think that they've done so much and so well in other areas of life: Why can't they beat this?

    Same reason they can't beat diabetes or cancer. It's an addiction, it's an illness, it's something you can't overcome yourself.

The same can often be said for changing minds.

How to Change Consumer Behavior

To see how removing all five barriers can work in concert, we turn to one of the most remarkable marketing campaigns in American history. It's hard to imagine a less compelling product: organ meat. But in 1943, the U.S. government had to convince its meat-loving populace to give up steak and to start frying up brains and kidneys—and to feel pride as they did it.

In January 1943, just over a year after the U.S. entered World War II, former president Herbert Hoover took to the pages of a food and nutrition magazine to deliver a stern warning about a unique threat: America's meat supply. "Meats and fats are just as much munitions in this war as are tanks and aeroplanes . . . ," he wrote . . . "Our farms are short of labor to care for livestock; and on top of it all we must furnish supplies to the British and the Russians."[13]

Food wasn't just sustenance; it was a matter of national security. Having led the U.S. Food Administration during World War I, Hoover understood that wars are often fought far from the battlefield. To have a chance at winning, the Allies needed their soldiers to be well-fed. And given that war had destroyed much of Europe's food supply, the United States needed to help provide for more than just their own fighting force.

But feeding all those soldiers meant cutting back on the home front. As more beef and pork were shipped overseas, meat soon joined cheese and butter as rationed food items.

This was a harsh blow to Americans' eating habits. Red meat was a prime source of energy, and particularly among the working class, its presence on the plate helped define what was seen as a proper meal.

Someone had to change Americans' minds about what types of meat to consume, shifting them from steaks and roasts and pork chops to less choice cuts that the soldiers wouldn't eat. Sweetbreads, hearts, liver, tongue, and other underutilized organ meats.

Aided by the burgeoning advertising industry, the government propaganda machine sprang to action. Lectures extolled organ meats' low cost and high nutritional value. Colorful posters and pamphlets appealed to patriotism. "Americans! Share the meat as a wartime necessity" and "Do with less so they'll have enough," they exhorted. By stretching food resources, ordinary Americans could help win the war.

The appeals were as inspiring as they were beautiful. Pictures of smiling wives carrying trays of liver loaf for their adoring husbands and sons. Red, white, and blue posters asking consumers whether they were doing all they could.

But for the most part, these efforts failed.

It wasn't that the public didn't care about the boys overseas. Or that they didn't understand that organ meats could be nutritious.

They both cared and understood, they just didn't shift their behavior. Blame inertia or squeamishness. Consumption of liver, tongue, and sweetbreads barely budged.

How could the government get American consumers to change their minds about organ meat?

As part of their efforts to shift Americans' meat consumption, the Department of Defense organized the inaugural Committee on Food Habits. And as part of that committee, they recruited psychologist Kurt Lewin.[14]

Lewin, often recognized as the founder of social psychology, studied in Germany and moved to the United States in 1933 to escape the Nazis' rise to power. He was a wizard at turning everyday problems into clever psychological experiments and saw how powerful psychological insight could be for improving the world.[15]

Before 1942, efforts to change public opinion tended to rely on education and emotion. "Present the facts clearly and correctly, the public *must* become interested, impressed, and persuaded."[16] Tell people what they should do, link it to something they care about, like patriotism, and they'll take action.

Lewin surveyed the situation and took a different tack. Incentives like eating nutritiously and being patriotic were fine, but they didn't seem like the most effective way to shift behavior. Rather than trying to persuade people or asking "What would convince Americans to eat organ meats?" Lewin asked a different question. One that is similar to the type of question we've been asking throughout the book: Why weren't people eating organ meats in the first place? What was stopping them?

After sifting through interviews, observations, and other

data, a few key obstacles or barriers to organ meat consumption emerged.

First was the format. Prior efforts had mostly told people what to do. Demanding that Americans "share the meat as a wartime necessity" appealed to patriotic duty, but it didn't make people feel like they had much choice in the matter. Which didn't make them rush to change their behavior.

Second, Americans were clearly wedded to what they were doing already. They loved steak and pork chops and all the other things they were used to eating, or were endowed with, and they didn't want to give them up.

Third was the size of the ask. Most early programs were all or nothing. They usually focused on only one type of organ meat and they encouraged eating it multiple times a week. A dramatic change that most families refused.

Fourth, there was a lot of uncertainty. Organ meats were just unfamiliar. Housewives didn't know what brains tasted like or how to prepare kidneys, and without that familiarity they weren't going to risk cooking it for their families.

Finally, most people didn't think organ meat was something folks like them ate. Some saw these cuts as useless leftovers that should be discarded. Others thought they were only appropriate for rural families or lower socioeconomic groups.

Armed with these insights, Lewin's committee stopped pushing harder with the same old ad campaigns. Instead they focused on removing the obstacles.

To reduce uncertainty, they tried to make organ meats more widely available, providing recipes and cooking tips wherever organ meats were sold. They suggested mixing it in as part of a larger dish of familiar foods that could be prepared the same way as regular meat. "Every husband will cheer for steak and kidney pie," one 1943 article suggested. Liver could be surreptitiously slipped into meat loaf so kids would dig in.

To shrink the distance between where people were and where the government wanted them to be, Lewin's team asked for less. Rather than demanding that Americans eat beef brains every day, they asked people to try organ meat once in a while. For variety, they could introduce it as filler in ground beef and sausages.

To ease endowment, Lewin's group surfaced the costs of inaction: how sticking with steaks and pork chops was hurting the troops.

And to reduce reactance and make the change feel more voluntary, Lewin tried small group discussions instead of lectures. Rather than telling homemakers what they *should* do, he brought them together and asked them to share their opinions. How could "housewives like yourself" overcome the obstacles that stood in the way.

These discussions provided corroborating evidence. They allowed homemakers to see and hear how other people were solving the same challenges: how mothers and spouses just like them were able to overcome their own uncertainties to help with the war effort.

At the end of the discussions, the group leaders took a quick poll. They asked women to raise their hands if they intended to try some of these new meats before the group's follow-up meeting.

And raise their hands they did.

The results were dramatic. Lewin's group discussions led to almost a third more women agreeing to serve organ meats.[17] But it was more than just that. Nationwide offal consumption rose by a third. Liver became a special treat.

Lewin's committee didn't just change consumer behavior; they did it in a situation where change seemed almost impossible. They showed it possible to take perhaps one of the least appealing products imaginable and to turn it into a delicacy in households across the country. And they did so using the exact same tools we've been talking about throughout the book.

Epilogue

The Israeli-Palestinian conflict is one of the most intractable issues of our time. Decades of failed negotiations and violent escalations have led to deep-seated mistrust and hate. Suicide bombings, rocket attacks, and other brutal confrontations have left citizens scared for their lives. Restricted movement, encroachment by settlers, and crushing economic sanctions have left many in poverty feeling like they have little rights or recourse.

Needless to say, animosity runs high. People see the other side as the enemy. An adversary that must be beaten using any means necessary. Trust between these rivals, let alone friendship, often seems impossible.

On a bright morning in Washington, DC, in 1993, however, there was hope. President Bill Clinton was addressing a distinguished group of attendees on the White House lawn, ushering in the public signing of the Oslo Accords. An agreement between Israeli prime minister Yitzhak Rabin and the chairman of the Palestinian Liberation Organization (PLO), Yasser Arafat.

It was a historic day for the Middle East. The first face-to-face agreement between the Israeli government and the PLO. In it, the PLO recognized Israel's right to exist and renounced violence. Israel, in turn, agreed to withdraw forces from parts of the Gaza Strip and West Bank and affirmed Palestinians' right to self-government. In addition to Rabin and Arafat, who eventually won the Nobel Peace Prize for their efforts, former U.S. presidents, ministers, and VIPs were there to show their support.

But in his speech, Clinton singled out a particular group of attendees. "In this entire assembly," asserted the president, "no one is more important."

That group wasn't made up of dignitaries or world leaders, former presidents or members of the press corps. In fact, in their green T-shirts and jeans, these individuals stood out rather incongruously among the cavalcade of luminaries.

They were a group of summer campers.

Seeds of Peace, as the camp is known, takes Egyptian, Israeli, and Palestinian teens and has them spend a few weeks together each summer at a lakeside retreat in southern Maine.

In addition to living in bunks, eating in mess halls, and engaging in all the normal paces of summer camp life, campers participate in dialogue sessions, attempting to talk through their differences.

Before Seeds of Peace, most campers have had no positive relationships with the other side. They're chosen by their respective governments to best represent their groups. Some teens are from the settlements, others are orthodox in their thinking if not in their religious views. Many are militant true believers, unshakable in their opinions.

"I walked into camp with a lot of hatred," said Habeeba, a young Egyptian who went through the program. "I wanted to prove a point and walk away. I wasn't looking to listen or learn."[*] As an Arab, she thought this was the patriotic thing to do. To show the Israelis that their government was bad, that they were living on someone else's land.

For many, the camp is a difficult experience. They feel like traitors, that they are betraying their countries by being there. Arabs are scared to sleep in the same cabin as Israelis, worried what will happen when they close their eyes. Israelis can't bear the thought of eating dinner at the same table as Palestinians.

Some activities, like art class, allow campers to interact with whomever they want. But others, like rock climbing, provide no way to avoid people you disagree with. "I obviously had to hold their hand if I wanted to move up," one camper explained. "It wasn't immediately melting away animosity; it was addressing it. It was hard, and I didn't like it."

And yet, over the three weeks these sworn enemies spent on the shores of Pleasant Lake, something fascinating happens.

They change.

In addition to rock climbing and art classes, campers also participate in what they call "Group Challenges." Making shapes with long ropes or doing other group activities.

Turning a rope into a circle or a star might seem easy, but even that is tough for a group that has spent the last couple of hours arguing over land rights or political representation. Campers don't want to work with the other side. Many are loud,

---

[*] Israeli attendees expressed the exact same sentiment.

assertive leaders who aren't interested in collaborating with the opposition.

One Group Challenge is a high-rope course. Campers are paired up, and one has to climb a tall telephone pole and follow guide ropes thirty feet above the ground. To make it even more challenging, they're blindfolded and all they have to rely on is the instructions from their partner.

They can't finish the challenge without working together. Sometimes both partners are blindfolded, and they have to find their way across the ropes together. Holding hands and talking each other through what they can touch but cannot see.

Habeeba remembers being paired with a tough Israeli. In the dialogue group, he had been so outspoken and steadfast that she couldn't establish a single point of common ground. She didn't trust him, and now, blindfolded, she had to completely depend on him for her balance, thirty feet up in the air.

She had a choice. Rely on someone she wasn't sure she could trust, or risk falling.

But as her partner guided her through the course, helping her through each step, she felt something shift. She found herself caring in a way she never thought possible. "He is just as human as me," she realized. "Up on the high ropes, I didn't care that he was Israeli and that I disagreed with him; I cared that we wouldn't fall."

This moment led to a broader realization. "Sometime in the past two weeks I had stopped judging people at camp by their nationality and started judging them individually, as people."

Habeeba wasn't alone. Researchers at the University of Chicago tracked the campers over time.[1] They measured the Israelis' and Palestinians' relationship with and attitudes toward one another.

The researchers found that the camp changed minds. By the end, campers' attitudes toward the other group improved. They liked and trusted the other side more and saw those onetime enemies as more similar to themselves. They also felt more optimistic about the likelihood of peace and more committed to working for it.

One might wonder whether these changes would just be short-lived. Maybe when teens returned to their conflict-torn homeland everything would revert back to where it was before.

But it didn't. Even a year after the camp had ended, former campers still felt more positive about the other group than they had felt before camp.

And these encounters drove more than just attitude change. For many campers, it marked the beginning of broader activism. Follow-up research[2] found that, as adults, a significant chunk of Seeds of Peace alumni are active in peace building and social change efforts, often ten or more years after initial participation.

President Clinton was right. These summer campers were the future of the peace process.

As with many conflicts, the media often uses a broad brush to depict each side. Some outlets portray Jews as manipulative monsters out to steal Arabs' homes and take their land. Others cast Palestinians as suicide bombers blindly following their faith and not to be trusted. With so many stereotypes and such xenophobia, it is easy to see the "enemy" as something other than human beings. As distant people with no faces.

But camp changes that. It helps kids realize that they actually have a lot in common with the other side. That they are fourteen, have crushes, and go to school, just like they themselves do.

"It made me see that the Israeli girl at my table really loves oranges, but she does not know how to peel them," Habeeba said. "I am going to help her peel them. You notice those things when you live with someone. You notice what kind of shampoos they use. Those are very human characteristics."

Seeds of Peace is an amazing organization. They've been a powerful catalyst for changing minds about the Israeli-Palestinian conflict and a variety of other contentious situations. But what is most powerful is how broadly their approach can be applied.

It's easy to read about a group like this and think that their situation is completely unique. After all, not many leaders can take their entire organization on a three-week summer camp. And few salespeople can convince their prospective clients to go on a rope course as a way to make a sale.

But while the program itself is unusual, the underlying reasons *why* it works are many of the same ones we've talked about throughout this book.

Seeds of Peace doesn't push Palestinians to be friends with Israelis or list more reasons why one side should trust the other. They don't make campers sit through endless lectures or implore them to do what's "right." Instead, they identify the key barriers preventing change and try to mitigate them.

Rather than trying to persuade people, they reduce **Reactance** by encouraging people to persuade themselves. Seeds of Peace has a desired destination in mind, but rather than forcing campers toward it, they allow for agency. They lay out a series of exercises and experiences that let campers pick their own paths to that outcome.

Instead of making a big ask right away, Seeds of Peace works to shrink the **Distance**. Rather than expecting opposing sides to be friends on day one, the camp starts by asking for less. Just sleep in the same cabin. Eat at the same table. Engage in the same activities and begin a dialogue. These activities help switch the field and find an unsticking point.

In this way, Seeds of Peace also reduces **Uncertainty**. Not only do they lower the up-front cost, allowing people who would normally fear one another to interact in a safe, neutral environment, they drive discovery. They don't sit back and hope the two sides interact; they create situations where interactions happen naturally. And the fact that the camp lasts for only a few short weeks makes things reversible. Worst case, campers will be back to their regular lives soon.

Finally, by giving campers multiple interactions with different outgroup members, they provide **Corroborating Evidence**. Even if Habeeba and an Israeli girl become friends, it's easy for Habeeba to see the one Israeli girl as unique. Sure, that girl is Israeli, but she's not like those *other* Israelis. She's different. And so Habeeba's trust toward Israelis in general doesn't really change. But when Habeeba has positive interactions with multiple Israelis, it's harder not to shift her attitudes toward them as a group. Meaning that she's much more likely to trust other Israelis she meets in the future.

Finding the Root

Behavioral scientist Kurt Lewin once noted, "If you want to truly understand something, try to change it." But the reverse is also true. To truly change something, you need to understand it.

Too often, as potential change agents we focus on ourselves.

We center on the outcome we're looking for or the change we're hoping to see. We're so blinded by the belief that we're right that we assume if we just provide more information, facts, or reasons, people will capitulate.

But more often than not, things don't budge. And by focusing so much on ourselves and what we want, we forget the most important part of change: understanding our audience.

Not just who they are, and how their needs might be different than ours, but—as we've talked about throughout the book—why they haven't changed already. What barriers or roadblocks are stopping them? What parking brakes are getting in the way?

The more we learn about what is preventing someone from changing, the easier it is to help. And to realize that things aren't as zero-sum as they may seem.

People think that, when changing minds, someone has to lose. Either they change or I'm worse off. That things are black-and-white and there are only two ways to go.

But the truth is often more complex.

Two chefs in a restaurant were fighting over the last orange left in the kitchen. It was late into dinner service, and both needed the orange for an important dish they were making, so they argued back and forth over who should have the right to use it.

Eventually, time was running out to get the dishes to the table, so they took a big kitchen knife and split the orange in half, leaving both with only half of what they needed.

But both chefs would have been better off if they understood the other's motivation. *Why* they needed the orange. Because one needed the juice for a sauce and the other needed the peel to bake a cake.

Whether cooking a dish, weeding a yard, or trying to get Israelis and Palestinians to see eye to eye, finding the root helps reach a better outcome.

Find those barriers, those parking brakes, and the rest will follow.

For a useful approach to identifying barriers,
see the Force Field Analysis appendix.

The Power of Catalysts

The story of Seeds of Peace highlights several important points.

First, anyone's mind can be changed. Whether it is about what to buy (Acura experience), how to vote (deep canvassing), or whether to quit smoking. Whether it's farmers adopting new innovations (hybrid corn), customers using new services (Dropbox), or kids eating their vegetables. Even in the unlikeliest of situations. Whether it's getting addicts to go to rehab, bank robbers to come out with their hands up, or conservatives to support transgender rights. Whether it's getting Israelis and Arabs to trust one another, meat eaters to become vegetarian, or companies to change their culture.

That's not to say it's easy to catalyze change, or that everyone's mind can be changed overnight. Take a look at big changes, and they're rarely that abrupt.

The Grand Canyon is one of the most spectacular gorges in the world. It's as long as the drive from Washington, DC, to Raleigh, North Carolina, and so deep that it takes over four hours to walk from the top to the bottom. It's so large it could swallow the state of Rhode Island, and so massive that it can create its own weather patterns.

How was this vast valley formed? One might think it was a massive earthquake or some earth-shattering event.

But it was nothing that sudden or momentous. It was water, slowly wearing down rock, over millions of years. A trickle that became a steady flow that eventually became the Colorado River.

Talk to someone who switched political parties, and it wasn't one eureka moment when everything suddenly clarified. Those make for great movies or great fiction, but they rarely happen in real life.

Instead, big changes tend to be more like the Grand Canyon: a slow and steady shift with many stages along the way. Talking to a professor in college or having a long debate with a roommate. Dealing with a surprising illness that changes how one sees the health care system, or struggling to identify with a new leader and the direction they've taken a party. Changes that happen over the period of years, not hours.

Particularly with bigger shifts, change takes weeks, months, or even years to occur. But by understanding why people change, and why they don't, catalysts make change more likely.

Second, when it comes to change, there's a better way. Not by pushing harder, or adding more energy, but by removing barriers to change. Reducing roadblocks. Being a catalyst.

Nafeez Amin didn't try to convince students to study more; he reduced reactance and got them to convince themselves that this was the best way to go. Dave Fleischer didn't pressure voters to support transgender rights; he shrank the distance and encouraged them to get there on their own. Greg Vecchi didn't tell mobsters to "come out with your hands up or we'll shoot"; he started with them, understood their needs, and used that to make them feel like coming out was their idea in the first place.

Whether it's about shifting minds, changing behavior, or inciting action, catalysts **REDUCE** roadblocks.

REACTANCE	When pushed, people push back. So rather than telling people what to do, or trying to persuade, catalysts allow for agency and encourage people to convince themselves.
ENDOWMENT	People are attached to the status quo. To ease endowment, catalysts surface the costs of inaction and help people realize that doing nothing isn't as costless as it seems.
DISTANCE	Too far from their backyard, people tend to disregard. Perspectives that are too far away fall in the region of rejection and get discounted, so catalysts shrink distance, asking for less and switching the field.
UNCERTAINTY	Seeds of doubt slow the winds of change. To get people to un-pause, catalysts alleviate uncertainty. Easier to try means more likely to buy.
CORROBORATING **E**VIDENCE	Some things need more proof. Catalysts find corroborating evidence, using multiple sources to help overcome the translation problem.

Whether you're trying to convince a client, change an organization, or disrupt the way an entire industry does business, think about what roadblocks are preventing change and how you can reduce them.

Here is a checklist that will help mitigate common barriers.

REDUCE REACTANCE	• How can you allow for agency? Like the truth campaign, encouraging people to chart their path to your destination? • Can you provide a menu? Like asking kids whether they want their broccoli or chicken first, can you use guided choices? • Like Smoking Kid, is there a gap between attitudes and behavior, and if so, how can you highlight it? • Rather than going straight for influence, have you started with understanding? Have you found the root? Like Greg Vecchi, built trust and use that to drive change?
EASE ENDOWMENT	• What is the status quo and what aspects make it attractive? • Are there hidden costs of sticking with it that people might not realize? • Like financial advisor Gloria Barrett, how can you surface the costs of inaction? • Like Cortés, or Sam Michaels in IT, how can you burn the ships to make it clear that going back isn't a feasible option? • Like Dominic Cummings and Brexit, can you frame new things as regaining a loss?

SHRINK DISTANCE	• How can you avoid the confirmation bias by staying out of the region of rejection? • Can you start by asking for less? Like the doctor who got the trucker to drink less soda, chunking the change and then asking for more? • Who falls in the movable middle and how can you use them to help convince others? • What would be a good unsticking point and how can you use it to switch the field? Like deep canvassing, by finding a dimension on which there is already common ground to bring people closer?
ALLEVIATE UNCERTAINTY	• How can you reduce uncertainty and get people to un-pause? Can you lower the barrier to trial? • Like Dropbox, can you leverage freemium? • Like Zappos, how can you reduce the up-front costs, using test drives, renting, sampling, or other approaches to make it easier for people to experience something themselves? • Rather than waiting for people to come to you, can you drive discovery? Like the Acura experience, by encouraging people who didn't know they might be interested to check it out? • Can you reduce friction on the back end by making things reversible? Like Street Tails Animal Rescue did with a two-week trial period, or as others do with lenient return policies?

FIND CORROBORATING
EVIDENCE

- Are you dealing with a pebble or
  a boulder? How expensive, risky,
  time-consuming, or controversial is
  the change you're asking people to
  make?
- How can you provide more proof?
  Like interventionists, by making sure
  people hear from multiple sources
  saying similar things?
- What similar but independent
  sources can you call on to help
  provide more evidence?
- How can you concentrate them
  close in time? Making sure people
  hear from multiple others in a short
  period?
- For larger-scale change, should
  you use a fire hose or a sprinkler?
  Concentrate scarce resources or
  spread them out?

But the last point is the most important one. And that is that anyone can be a catalyst.

You don't have to be a slick talker or have the best PowerPoint deck. You don't have to have a huge advertising budget or work for a big organization. And you don't have to have twenty years of domain expertise, know how to speak with your hands, or be the most charismatic person in the room.

Jacek Nowak was struggling to get buy-in from senior management. He was working in an industry, banking, that is known for being reticent to change. And he was trying to get them to do something about customer experience that was in some senses the antithesis of what they were used to. But by lowering the barrier to trial and driving discovery, he helped management experience the value of what he was suggesting and ultimately adopt his suggestions.

Chuck Wolfe was competing against one of the largest industries in the world, whose budget dwarfed his by more than a thousandfold. And getting teens to quit smoking was something that dozens of organizations had been trying to do for decades, without much success. But by laying out the truth rather than telling teens what to do, he was able to turn the tide. By letting them be active participants rather than passive bystanders, Chuck made them feel like they were in control. He reduced reactance and got teens to convince themselves.

Nick Swinmurn needed a way to help a small start-up get off the ground. Shoesite.com was running out of money and they needed to change consumer behavior—fast. But rather than trying to convince people or spending funds they didn't have on splashy ads, they removed the roadblocks. They used free shipping (and returns) to let potential customers experience the offering firsthand. By lowering the barrier to trial, Zappos reduced risk, alleviated uncertainty, and built a billion-dollar business. And along the way, helped usher in the world of online shopping we're all so familiar with today.

Normal people, in difficult situations, who became catalysts. By finding the root, and removing barriers, they were able to change minds.

Everyone has something they want to change. Politicians want to change voting behavior and marketers want to build their customer base. Employees want to change their bosses' perspectives and leaders want to transform organizations. Spouses want to change their partners' minds and parents want to shift their children's behavior. Start-ups want to change industries and nonprofits want to change the world.

Throughout this book, we've examined cutting-edge science of change. Looking at how, when, and why people shift their beliefs, alter their actions, and adopt new and different perspectives.

By being a catalyst, and working to REDUCE roadblocks, you, too, can change anyone's mind.

Acknowledgments

Thanks to Greg Vecchi, Dave Fleischer, Chuck Wolfe, Max Doroodian, Phil Laduca, Stefan Burford, Fred Mossler, Andy Arnold, Ned Lazarus, David Broockman, Nafeez Amin, Jacek Nowak, Kimberly Culmone, Sebastian Buck, Michael Weisser, Michael Hone, Priyanca Ford, Edward Scerbo, Brendan Bosch, Hillary Law, Carolina Hernandez, Diego Martinez, Michael Hammelburger, Silvia Branscom, Katherine Devore, Sandra Hamorsky, Matt Shapiro, Phil Kim, Deb Levy, Jiawei Li, Habeeba, and all the other people who took the time to share their stories. Thanks to Richard Rhorer for the email and germ of an idea that started this whole thing, to Jon Cox for stewarding the manuscript through the process, to Alice LaPlante for tightening things, and to Jon Karp for helpful feedback. Thanks to Nicole Beurkens, Kristen Lindquist, Kurt Gray, Jillian Dempsey, Alex Miller, Mike and Jess Christian, Alexander Berger, Louise Stanger, Patrick Jeffs, Justin Etkin, Carey Morewedge, Juliana Schroeder, Justin Etkin, Ned Lazarus, Fred Irby, and Gabe Adams for answering domain-specific questions on a range of topics. I'm sure my requests came out of left field, but you answered them patiently and thoughtfully. Thanks to George Ferridge, Jiawei Li, Sally Shin, Theo Damiani, William Murray, Catherine Wang, and other research assistants for help collecting information for various parts of the book. Thanks to Caroline and Lilly for loving to read, to Brittany Hull for taking such wonderful care of Jasper, and to Travis and the UNC lunchtime basketball for providing a nice outlet between bouts of writing (hopefully this explains why I'm always late). To Nipsey Hussle for all the support over the years, RIP. And to Bobby Francis, for having the vision to guide the journey. Thanks to Megan Costello, Shambavi Krishnamurthi, Jamie Joseph, Lindsay Pistor, Zachary Boven, Jason Peterson, Jill Ni, Alex Capretta, Josh March, Aston Hamilton, Amanda Morrison, Margaret Souther, Falon Dominguez, Anthony Beshay, and Julia Moon for taking the time during a busy year to read various drafts and provide helpful feedback. You kept pushing on how the ideas could be applied, which helped immensely. Thanks to Jim Levine: I could not have done this without you and always appreciate your guidance. (One day I hope to be as Zen about everything as you are.) To my parents, for all the articles and thoughts and moral support.

Appendix:
Active Listening

Starting with understanding is a helpful way to find the root and understand why someone hasn't changed already. And active listening facilitates that process. Listening is important, but it's often equally important to ask the right questions and to show people that you're listening. To signal that you are paying attention and tracking what they are saying. Here are a few key tactics:

Use Minimal Encouragers

One way to show someone you are listening is to demonstrate through your body language and verbal responses that you are focused on what is being said. This can include nodding your head, leaning forward, or watching the person's eyes, as well as phrases like "Yes," "Uh-huh," and "Okay, I see." While such assent words or phrases may seem inconsequential, they're actually the glue that holds conversation together. When presenters don't get any response or feedback from their audience, they not only enjoy it less, they do a worse job overall.[1]

Ask Open-ended Questions

Questions get discussion going and build trust. Looking at a range of situations, from getting-to-know-you conversations to speed dating, people who ask more questions are liked more.[2] Questions also help collect useful information so people can better understand their conversation partners.

But not all questions are equally good. Why questions ("Why didn't you take out the trash?"), for example, can make people defensive or feel like they are being interrogated. Yes-no questions, or those that encourage one-word answers ("Do you have a gun?"), are also less effective because they fail to advance the conversation.

Open-ended questions ("Can you tell me more about that?" or "Wow, how did that happen?") not only show people you're listening but generate details and information that can be helpful later.

Harness Effective Pauses

Pauses harness the power of silence. Silence can be uncomfortable, so people tend to fill in conversational space. Hostage negotiators use pauses to get subjects to speak up and provide additional information, particularly when they think asking a question might derail things. Rather than asking a follow-up question, they'll be quiet and let the suspect fill in the dead air.

Pauses also help focus attention. Pausing just before or after saying something important breeds anticipation and encourages listeners to focus on what the communicator is saying. President Obama was famous for this. His campaign slogan "Yes, we can" was often delivered with a pause in between, as in "Yes . . . we can." In his 2008 election night speech, his most stirring sentence contained ten of these pauses: "If there is anyone out there . . . who still doubts . . . that America is a place . . . where all things are possible, . . . who still wonders . . . if the dream of our Founders . . . is alive in our time, . . . who still questions . . . the power of our democracy, . . . tonight . . . is your answer." Strategically pausing helps make points and hold attention.

Reflect What You Heard

Mirroring involves repeating the last few words of what someone said to show you're listening and engaged. Particularly if someone is feeling emotional, it encourages them to keep talking and gives them the opportunity to vent. If someone says, "I'm so annoyed that our supplier is always a day or two late," for example, one could respond, "They're always a day or two late?" Mirroring builds liking and affiliation while keeping the conversation flowing.

Rather than repeating exactly what was said, paraphrasing involves restating someone's meaning using your own words. This shows not only that you're listening but that you truly understand what was being conveyed.

Label Emotions

Changing minds is often as much about emotion as information. Facts and figures are fine, but if you don't understand the underlying emotional issues, it's hard to get people to move. Emotional labeling helps identify the issues and feelings that are driving someone's behavior. Statements like "You sound angry" or "You seem frustrated" help show that you're listening and trying to understand. Even if the emotion is misidentified, the response provides background that helps identify the root issue.

Appendix:
Applying Freemium

Freemium can be a powerful business model, both to attract new users and to transition them into paying ones. But the success of the model hinges on *how much* is being given away.

Say Dropbox gave away only a small amount of storage before a message popped up saying you had to pay to get more space. Most people would probably find this quite annoying. They'd barely have started using the service before being hit up for money, and without having spent enough time using it, they probably wouldn't find the offering valuable enough to keep paying. They'd likely go elsewhere.

On the other end, giving away too much can also be dangerous. The *New York Times* website used to provide twenty articles a month for free. But that was so much free content that not enough users were converting to premium. Few people read that many articles a month, so most people had no reason to upgrade.

The key, then, is giving away enough to generate a positive, upgrade-worthy experience, but not so much that no one ever needs more.

Indeed, after analyzing their usage rates, the *Times* eventually lowered the number of free articles to ten. Still a significant chunk, but enough to encourage high-volume users to transition to the premium offering.

It all comes down to (1) how many new users sign up, and (2) the conversion rate, or percentage of them that upgrade. If user growth is stagnating, the offering is not enticing enough, so more or better things need to be included in the free version. If users are flooding in but few are upgrading, the opposite may be true: the free version is too generous, or the premium version isn't clearly differentiated enough to make upgrading seem worthwhile.

Beyond how much to give away, though, another important question is what *dimension* to limit.

The *New York Times* and Dropbox limit capacity, providing a certain number of free articles a month or a certain amount of free storage. Gyms and classes limit time, offering a thirty-day free trial or the first class free. And video chat clients, Pandora, and games like Candy Crush limit features (e.g., who can present, the presence of ads, or what level users can access), making some but not all of the capabilities available right away.

When deciding which dimension to limit, the solution comes back to uncertainty. What experience will provide enough certainty that it is worth paying to upgrade?

If users don't discover the value of certain aspects or dimensions right away, limiting features makes the most sense. Alternatively, if users get the best experience from having access to all the features right away, then limiting time or capacity may be a better option.

Appendix:
Force Field Analysis

Parking brakes, or barriers, come in many forms. But one of the biggest challenges in removing roadblocks is identifying them in the first place.

Take a new travel app that promises to save time and money. Typically the pitch would focus on how great the app is. How it can cut planning time in half or save you 25 percent on hotels and flights.

But there are various hurdles that might hinder adoption. Some consumers may not realize they have a problem. Others might not understand the solution (i.e., how it will save money) or believe that it's true (i.e., that the app will actually do what it promises). Still more might be worried that it will have limited options or be difficult to use.

Just like a doctor prescribing medicine, without understanding the problem, it's hard to suggest the right solution. If people don't understand how the app saves money, then walking them through that pitch may be helpful. But if the barrier is that they think it will have limited options or will be difficult to use, a different approach is needed. Claiming the app saves money won't address these concerns. It's like prescribing a finger splint for a toothache.

Is it easier to carpet-bomb all potential clients with the same email? Certainly. Is it faster to use the same pitch when trying to change different departments in an organization? Without a doubt.

But while those one-size-fits-all approaches might seem like they save time, they're much less effective. Which means returning again and again with new appeals.

Instead, we need to find the root. Identify the core issue or barrier that's preventing action.

One technique experts often use is called a force field analysis. It's a framework for analyzing the various factors, or forces, at work in a given situation and using that analysis to facilitate change.

The first step in any force field analysis is defining the change. Identify the goal, desired state, or thing you are hoping will happen. The client signs a long-term contract. Management funds that new initiative. Your spouse stops complaining about their in-laws.

Then identify the driving forces or existing factors that are encouraging change. Some may be internal, or things within the person or organization: the client liked our work so far or the project fits with management's broader vision. Others may be external, or things outside the person or organization: the client's company tends to prefer long-term deals, or if the project goes well, the experience can be used across the organization.

Finally, and most importantly, start to identify the restrainers. The barriers or hurdles preventing change from happening. Just as with drivers, restraining forces can be internal or external. In

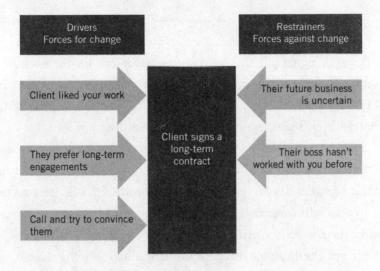

the case of clients, they may be uncertain about what their own businesses will look like in a year or two. In the case of a new initiative, there may be concerns about staffing.*

One way to spot barriers is to think about the past and present rather than the future. As we've discussed, instead of asking what *would* encourage change, ask why things haven't changed *already*. Why hasn't the desired shift already occurred. What's preventing it? What existing factors have prevented it from happening by now?

Asking questions, like who is against the change, and identifying the costs and risks involved is also useful. What does the client seem worried about? What concerns or motivations might keep management from supporting the new initiative?

---

* An optional step is to assign weights. For each driving or restraining force you've identified, think about how weak or strong it is. Things that have greater influence should get larger numbers, and things with weaker influence should have smaller numbers.

Say you're trying to get your teenage son to eat healthier. Rather than just nagging him more or reminding him that he should lay off the chips and eat more vegetables, a force field analysis highlights some more effective solutions.

The desired change is clear: he starts eating healthier. In addition to your constant reminders that he should eat more vegetables (external), drivers might include things like he's trying to lose weight (internal) and that he wants to get faster so he can make the soccer team (internal).

Given all those positive forces for change, why hasn't he started eating healthier already? Maybe he thinks healthy food tastes bad (internal). Or he's always rushing from school to after-school activities and junk food is easy to grab (external). Or he's trying to express his independence, so whatever you ask, he does the opposite.

Given these restrainers, or barriers to change, it's no surprise that nagging him isn't working. Or that reminding him to lay off chips has backfired. Pushing harder won't reduce these barriers or make them disappear.

Laying out the situation this way makes it easier to catalyze change. Because it highlights alternate paths to the same goal. Not by being more convincing, but by removing roadblocks. Lowering the taste barrier by making cauliflower mac and cheese. Solving the time crunch by putting things like bags of baby carrots in the fridge that he can easily grab and go.

Recognizing restrainers helps find the roots(s). And identify the parking brakes. Facilitating the path to change.

Notes

Introduction
1. Ireland, Carol A., and Gregory M. Vecchi (2009), "The Behavioral Influence Stairway Model (BISM): A Framework for Managing Terrorist Crisis Situations?" *Behavioral Sciences of Terrorism and Political Aggression* 1, no. 3, 203–18. Vecchi, Gregory M., Vincent B. Van Hasselt, and Stephen J. Romano (2005), "Crisis (Hostage) Negotiation: Current Strategies and Issues in High-Risk Conflict Resolution," *Aggression and Violent Behavior* 10, no. 5, 533–51. Noesner, Gary W., and Mike Webster (1997), "Crisis Intervention: Using Active Listening Skills in Negotiations," *FBI Law Enforcement Bulletin* 66, 13.
2. To preserve anonymity, pseudonyms are used for some of the people discussed.

1. Reactance
1. Fellows, J. L., A. Trosclair, E. K. Adams, and C. C. Rivera (2002), "Annual Smoking-Attributable Mortality, Years of Potential Life Lost, and Economic Cost—United States 1995–1999," Centers for Disease Control and Prevention (accessed August 17, 2019), available at https://www.cdc.gov/mmwr/preview/mmWrhtml/mm5114 a2.htm.
2. Centers for Disease Control and Prevention (July 9, 2010), "Cigarette Use Among High School Students—United States, 1991–2009," *Morbidity and Mortality Weekly Report* 1, no. 26, 797–801.

3. Hanson, Glen, Peter Venturelli, and Annette Fleckenstein (2011), *Drugs and Society* (Burlington, MA: Jones & Bartlett).

4. It's worth noting that some people who "participated" in the Tide Pod Challenge did so ironically. YouTubers did it for views or poked fun at the challenge without actually participating. A pizzeria in Brooklyn, for example, released a Tide Pod pizza topped with cheese dyed to look like the Pods. But some of the younger viewers may not have realized that many people were joking, and they actually ended up in the hospital.

5. Decades of research on reactance have found that people seek things or avoid them to assert their threatened freedom. Some examples include: Bensley, Lillian Southwick, and Rui Wu (1991), "The Role of Psychological Reactance in Drinking Following Alcohol Prevention Messages," *Journal of Applied Social Psychology* 21, no. 13, 1111–24. Wolf, Sharon, and David A. Montgomery (1977), "Effects of Inadmissible Evidence and Level of Judicial Admonishment to Disregard on the Judgments of Mock Jurors," *Journal of Applied Social Psychology* 7, no. 3, 205–19. Wong, Norman C. H., Kylie J. Harrison, and Lindsey Harvell-Bowman (2015), "When the Death Makes You Smoke: A Terror Management Perspective on the Effectiveness of Cigarette On-Pack Warnings," Studies in Media and Communication (accessed August 17, 2019), available at https://www.researchgate.net/publication/282519431_Reactance _and_Public_Health_Messages_The_Unintended_Dangers_of _Anti-tobacco_PSAs.

6. Rodin, Judith, and Ellen J. Langer (1977), "Long-Term Effects of a Control-Relevant Intervention with the Institutionalized Aged," *Journal of Personality and Social Psychology* 35, no. 12, 897. Langer, Ellen J., and Judith Rodin, "The Effects of Choice and Enhanced Personal Responsibility for the Aged: A Field Experiment in an Institutional Setting," *Journal of Personality and Social Psychology* 34, no. 2, 191. While the mortality result used a relatively small sample size and should be interpreted with caution, the other findings have been conceptually replicated in a variety of other domains.

7. Botti, Simona, Kristina Orfali, and Sheena S. Iyengar (2009), "Tragic Choices: Autonomy and Emotional Responses to Medical Decisions," *Journal of Consumer Research* 36, no. 3, 337–52.

8. Brehm (1966) provides some of the early work on reactance. Worchel and Brehm (1970) demonstrate the idea of a boomerang effect in response to certain persuasive messages. Brehm, Jack W.

(1966), *A Theory of Psychological Reactance* (Oxford, UK: Academic Press). Worchel, Stephen, and Jack W. Brehm (1970), "Effect of Threats to Attitudinal Freedom as a Function of Agreement with the Communicator," *Journal of Personality and Social Psychology*, 14, no. 1, 18.

9. Dozens of studies have shown that reactance makes people less likely to comply to requests in a range of domains. Children who thought an ad was trying to persuade them trusted the ad less and liked the product less (Robertson and Rossiter, 1974). When doctors spoke more authoritatively (e.g., telling patients that they needed to follow their advice or things would get worse) rather than treating the relationship like a partnership (e.g., "We're in this together to help you feel better"), patients were slower to fill their prescriptions, skipped doses, and were more likely not to take all their medicine (Fogarty and Youngs, 2000). And providing people with recommendations (Fitzsimons and Lehmann, 2004) can lead them to feel the opposite. Robertson, Thomas S., and John R. Rossiter (1974), "Children and Commercial Persuasion: An Attribution Theory Analysis," *Journal of Consumer Research* 1, no. 1, 13–20. Fogarty, Jeanne S., and George A. Youngs Jr. (2000), "Psychological Reactance as a Factor in Patient Noncompliance with Medication Taking: A Field Experiment," *Journal of Applied Social Psychology* 30, no. 11, 2365–91. Fitzsimons, Gavan J., and Donald R. Lehmann (2004), "Reactance to Recommendations: When Unsolicited Advice Yields Contrary Responses," *Marketing Science* 23, no. 1, 82–94.

10. Fransen, Marieke L., Edith G. Smit, and Peeter W. J. Verlegh (2015), "Strategies and Motives for Resistance to Persuasion: An Integrative Framework," *Frontiers in Psychology* 6, 1201.

11. Givel, Michael S., and Stanton A. Glantz (1999), "Tobacco Industry Political Power and Influence in Florida from 1979 to 1999," working paper, University of California, San Francisco: Center for Tobacco Control Research and Education.

12. Another reason truth was so effective was that it cleverly reframed the choice to smoke. Whereas smoking had been seen as an act of rebellion (e.g., *Who cares about those health warnings? I'm tough*), the truth campaign reframed it as an act of conformity, of gullibly giving in to the wishes of powerful tobacco companies. Rather than trying to defeat reactance by pushing harder or pretending it didn't exist, truth simply harnessed it and pointed it in a different direction. Want to react against something? It's the *cigarette companies*

you should react against. They're the real ones trying to influence your behavior. In exposing the manipulation, insidiousness, and power of Big Tobacco, truth short-circuited the pro-smoking ads and defused their power.

13. A favorite application of guided choices comes from Sandra Boynton's children's book *Night-Night, Little Pookie*. Pookie's mom is trying to get him dressed for bed and gives Pookie a choice between two pairs of pajama tops and bottoms: "So tonight will you wear the pajamas with cars? Or do you prefer the pajamas with stars?" Pookie, ever the wily pig, goes with the stars top and the cars bottom and replies, "Stars AND cars."

14. Note that this also helps to reach so-called Pareto efficiency: letting potential hires choose between options equally acceptable to the boss while simultaneously allowing them to improve the outcome for themselves.

15. Even just acknowledging resistance can be helpful. When random pedestrians were asked to give money to feed a parking meter, around half agreed. But when that request was accompanied by an acknowledgment that the person might not want to ("I know you might not want to, but would you be willing to give me some money for the meter?"), almost everyone was willing to help. Acknowledging that people might not want to do something validates their autonomy. It highlights that, rather than being forced to do something, they are making a free choice. Recognizing the resistance, and honoring it, makes people more willing to change.

16. A financial advisor had a tough client who just wasn't putting enough money away for retirement. The advisor kept telling the man to save, but he just wasn't doing it. She sent him articles extolling the benefits of compound interest and chart after chart demonstrating the value of taking action immediately, but nothing seemed to persuade her client to save more. Eventually she just asked him flat out, "Aren't you hoping to retire at some point?" "Of course," he said. "What age are you hoping to be able to retire?" "Around 65," he replied. "Okay, and what are you hoping retirement will look like?" The client replied that he wanted to be able to play golf and travel and kick back and relax a little bit. "Do you know how much you need to have saved at that point to live that way?" she asked. He said he didn't, so they started to work through the numbers. They agreed that he needed around $1.5 million to retire the way he wanted to. But rather than stop there, the advisor went a step further. She opened up a retirement calculator and started

working backwards. Given her client's income and the amount he could be saving, he needed to have a million in the bank by the time he was sixty. Which meant having $500,000 in the bank by age fifty-four. Which meant at least $100,000 more than he currently had in only a couple of years. He gulped, but after that meeting, he started more than doubling the amount he was saving each month. Helping him clearly see the difference between where he was and where he wanted to go encouraged him to take action.

17. Dickerson, Chris Ann, Ruth Thibodeau, Elliot Aronson, and Dayna Miller (1992), "Using Cognitive Dissonance to Encourage Water Conservation," *Journal of Applied Social Psychology* 22, no. 11, 841–54.

18. For more about the Weissers and their story, see Watterson, Kathryn (2012), *Not by the Sword: How a Cantor and His Family Transformed a Klansman* (Lincoln, NE: University of Nebraska Press).

2. Endowment

1. Hartman, R. S., M. J. Doane, and C.-K. Woo (1991), "Consumer Rationality and the Status Quo," *Quarterly Journal of Economics* 106, no. 1, 141–62.

2. For work on status quo bias, see Samuelson, W., and R. Zeckhauser (1988), "Status Quo Bias in Decision Making," *Journal of Risk and Uncertainty* 1, no. 1, 7–59. Kahneman, Daniel, Jack L. Knetsch, and Richard H. Thaler (1991), "Anomalies: The Endowment Effect, Loss Aversion, and Status Quo Bias," *Journal of Economic Perspectives* 5, no. 1, 193–206.

3. Katzenbach, Jon R., Ilona Steffen, and Caroline Kronley (2012), "Cultural Change That Sticks," *Harvard Business Review*, July–August.

4. Morewedge, Carey K., and Colleen E. Giblin (2015), "Explanations of the Endowment Effect: An Integrative Review," *Trends in Cognitive Sciences* 19, no. 6, 339–48.

5. Strahilevitz, Michal A., and George Loewenstein (1998), "The Effect of Ownership History on the Valuation of Objects," *Journal of Consumer Research* 25, no. 3, 276–89. Reb, Jochen, and Terry Connolly (2007), "Possession, Feelings of Ownership, and the Endowment Effect," *Judgment and Decision Making* 2, no. 2, 107.

6. Just showing that sellers value something more than buyers does not make it clear whether sellers overvalue what they have or buyers undervalue what they don't. But some clever studies have disentangled these two possibilities. In one study, for example, in addition to regular mug buyers and mug sellers, a third group of

people were given a coffee mug and then asked how much they would be willing to pay to buy a second, identical mug. If it was just that people undervalue what they don't have, these owner-buyers should value the mug like regular mug buyers. After all, they don't yet have the second mug; they're just bidding on it. But instead, researchers found that these individuals valued the mug as much as regular mug sellers. This indicates that, in addition to devaluing things they don't have, people also overvalue what they have already (or things that are similar).

7. Britton, Diana (2015), "The Loss Aversion Coefficient," Wealth Management.com, February 10, http://www.wealthmanagement .com/equities/loss-aversion-coefficient. Different papers have found varying estimates of the coefficient of loss aversion. Novemsky and Kahneman (2005) suggest a value of around 2. Reviewing prior work, Abdellaoui, Bleichrodt, and L'Haridon (2008) suggest values between 1.43 and 4.99. See Gachter, Simon, Eric J. Johnson, and Andreas Herrmann (2007), "Individual-Level Loss Aversion in Riskless and Risky Choices," IZA working paper 2961, for a review.

8. Harvard Business School Case #2069, "Mountain Man Brewing Company: Bringing the Brand to Light."

9. When facing a difficult decision (e.g., whether or not to have surgery), research even suggests people paradoxically prefer, and feel better with, objectively worse news (e.g., "You have a severe injury" rather than "You have a moderate injury"), because it helps them know what to do. If they know the injury is severe, there's less doubt about whether something needs to be done about it.

10. For a nice discussion of this, see Gilbert, D. T., M. D. Lieberman, C. K. Morewedge, and T. D. Wilson, (2004), "The Peculiar Longevity of Things Not So Bad," *Psychological Science* 15, 14–19.

11. Collins, J. C. (2001), *Good to Great: Why Some Companies Make the Leap . . . and Others Don't* (New York: HarperBusiness).

12. While some think that he burned the vessels, others have argued that he ran them aground.

13. Some have argued that this number is potentially misleading, because it doesn't take into account the rebate that is applied. That said, the revised number is still £234 million a week. This money is used for agricultural subsidies, research, and grants to poorer regions, and some of it does return to the UK; but even when these return payments are taken into account, the outflow is still around £160 million a week.

3. Distance

1. Fleischer, David (2018), "How to fight prejudice through policy conversations," TEDxMidAtlantic, https://www.ted.com/talks/david _fleischer_how_to_fight_prejudice_through_policy_conversa tions.

2. Bail, Christopher, Lisa Argyle, Taylor Brown, John Bumpus, Hao-han Chen, M. B. Hunzaker, Jaemin Lee, Marcus Mann, Friedolin Merhout, and Alexander Volfovsky (2018), "Exposure to Opposing Views on Social Media Can Increase Political Polarization," *Proceedings of the National Academy of Sciences* 115, no. 37, 9216–21.

3. Nyhan, Brendan, Jason Reifler, Sean Richey, and Gary L. Freed (2014), "Effective Messages in Vaccine Promotion: A Randomized Trial," *Pediatrics* 133, no. 4 (April).

4. Rather than clarifying the falsehood, evidence that Iraq didn't have weapons of mass destruction made some people more likely to believe they did. Giving conservatives evidence that tax cuts don't increase government revenues made them believe it more fervently. And rather than turning them away, negative information about a political candidate people already liked increased their support. Redlawsk, David P. (2002), "Hot Cognition or Cool Consideration? Testing the Effects of Motivated Reasoning on Political Decision Making," *Journal of Politics* 64, no. 4, 1021–44.

5. Hovland, Carl I., O. J. Harvey, and Muzafer Sherif (1957), "Assimilation and Contrast Effects in Reactions to Communication and Attitude Change," *Journal of Abnormal and Social Psychology* 55, no. 2, 244–52.

6. In the decades that followed, dozens of studies have shown similar findings. Students were persuaded by communications about fraternities that fell within their latitude of acceptance. But if the appeals were outside their latitudes, the communications backfired and shifted attitudes in the opposite direction. Atkins, A. L., Kay K. Deaux, and James Bieri (1967), "Latitude of Acceptance and Attitude Change: Empirical Evidence for a Reformulation," *Journal of Personality and Social Psychology* 6, no. 1 (May), 47–54. Political appeals encouraging people to support either Democratic or Republican candidates worked among people who held similar views but backfired among people who held the opposite perspective. Sherif, C. W., M. Sherif, and R. E. Nebergall (1965), *Attitude and Attitude Change: The Social Judgment–Involvement Approach* (Philadelphia: W. B. Saunders).

7. Hastorf, Albert H., and Hadley Cantril (1954), "They Saw a

Game: A Case Study," *Journal of Abnormal and Social Psychology* 49, no. 1, 129.

8. In a more recent version (Kahan, Hoffman, Braman, Peterman, and Rachlinski [2012]. "'They Saw a Protest': Cognitive Illiberalism and the Speech-Conduct Distinction," *Stanford Law Review*, Vol. 64), law professors showed people a video of a protest and asked them about the conduct of both the police and the demonstrators. Things like whether the police had violated the demonstrators' rights and whether protesters obstructed pedestrians. Different groups of viewers were told different things about the protest. Some were told that the demonstrators were protesting outside an abortion clinic; others were told that the demonstrators were protesting the military's "Don't ask, don't tell" policy outside a recruitment center. This detail completely changed how viewers interpreted things. When they thought they were watching an anti-abortion protest, viewers who were against abortion themselves thought the protesters acted fairly. But when military supporters watched the same video, thinking they were watching an anti-military protest, they thought the same protesters were screaming in the faces of pedestrians and behaving inappropriately.

9. Lord, Charles G., Lee Ross, and Mark R. Lepper (1979), "Biased Assimilation and Attitude Polarization: The Effects of Prior Theories on Subsequently Considered Evidence," *Journal of Personality and Social Psychology* 37, no. 11 (November), 2098–109.

10. Nickerson, Raymond S. (1998), "Confirmation Bias: A Ubiquitous Phenomenon in Many Guises," *Review of General Psychology* 2, no. 2, 175. Also see Brock, T. C., and J. L. Balloun (1967), "Behavioral Receptivity to Dissonant Information," *Journal of Personality and Social Psychology* 6, no. 4, 413–28.

11. Sherif, Sherif, and Nebergall (1965), *Attitude and Attitude Change: The Social Judgment-Involvement Approach*.

12. Kalla, Joshua L., and David E. Broockman (2017), "The Minimal Persuasive Effects of Campaign Contact in General Elections: Evidence from 49 Field Experiments," *American Political Science Review* (September 28). While this work didn't find an overall persuasive effect, they did note the value of advertising and campaign contact in helping increase turnout, which can also impact elections.

13. Eagly, Alice H., and Kathleen Telaak (1972), "Width of the Latitude of Acceptance as a Determinant of Attitude Change," *Journal of Personality and Social Psychology* 23, no. 3, 388.

14. Rogers, Todd, and David Nickerson (2013), "Can Inaccurate

Beliefs About Incumbents Be Changed? And Can Reframing Change Votes?," working paper, Harvard University.

15. Freedman, Jonathan L., and Scott C. Fraser (1966), "Compliance Without Pressure: The Foot-in-the-Door Technique," *Journal of Personality and Social Psychology* 4, no. 2, 195.

16. Our dog has her own version of "Ask for less." She's never been allowed on the couch, and when she'd jump on as a puppy, we'd gently push her off and tell her no. So rather than jumping on all the way, she started putting just one front paw on the couch. If no one corrected her, she'd add a second front paw, and a back paw, and so on, until she was finally all the way up.

17. Greene, Bob (2004), *Get with the Program* (New York: Simon & Schuster).

18. Broockman, David E., and Joshua L. Kalla (2016), "Durably Reducing Transphobia: A Field Experiment on Door-to-door Canvassing, " *Science* 352, no. 6282 (April), 220–24.

19. Fleischer, David (2018), "How to fight prejudice through policy conversations," TEDxMidAtlantic, https://www.ted.com/talks/david _fleischer_how_to_fight_prejudice_through_policy_conversations.

20. Deep canvassing also encourages what psychologists call "active processing." Rather than being a passive listener, voters are encouraged to do most of the talking. Virginia not only asked Gustavo what his opinion was, she also asked him to explain why he felt that way—not in a judgmental manner but as a friend might to understand where someone is coming from. This encouraged effortful reflection and wrestling with the complex nature of the issues. Not just going, "Yeah, yeah, prejudice is bad, got it," but truly engaging with the topic in a thoughtful way.

21. Perspective taking often fails (i.e., fails to increase accuracy when predicting another person's thoughts, feelings, or attitudes). See Eyal, T., M. Steffel, and N. Epley (2018), "Perspective mistaking: Accurately understanding the mind of another requires getting perspective, not taking perspective," *Journal of Personality and Social Psychology* 114, 547–71.

4. Uncertainty

1. Gneezy, Uri, John A. List, and George Wu (2006), "The Uncertainty Effect: When a Risky Prospect Is Valued Less Than Its Worst Possible Outcome," *Quarterly Journal of Economics* 121, no. 4, 1283–309.

2. While the two are often used colloquially to mean similar things, "risk" and "uncertainty" have slightly different technical meanings.

Scientists use the term "risk" to describe situations where the outcome itself is unknown but the probability of different outcomes is known. Flip a coin, and you expect the chance of it landing either heads or tails is 50 percent. You don't know for certain whether it will be heads or tails on any given toss, but you know the chance is 50 percent. Uncertainty, in contrast, is used to describe situations where the likelihood of different outcomes is also unknown. What's my favorite color? Not only do you not know the answer, you don't even know the chance it could be different options.

3. While this example is related to the inertia discussion from the introduction, it is different in some important ways. Rather than comparing the expected value of a loss with the expected value of a gain, for example, here both gift cards are a gain; people are just unsure which gain they will get.

4. While a number of papers have documented the cost of uncertainty (Andreoni and Sprenger [2011]; Gneezy et al. [2006]; Newman and Mochon [2012]; Simonsohn [2009]; Wang et al. [2013]; Yang et al. [2013]), some recent work (Mislavsky and Simonsohn [2018]) suggests that at least a portion of the effect may be a result of those studies confounding uncertainty and unexplained transaction features. That said, even this work finds some evidence that uncertainty may decrease valuation, even if the effect is not as large as that observed in prior studies. Andreoni, James, and Charles Sprenger (2011), "Uncertainty Equivalents: Testing the Limits of the Independence Axiom," working paper, National Bureau of Economic Research, No. w17342. Newman, George E., and Daniel Mochon (2012), "Why Are Lotteries Valued Less? Multiple Tests of a Direct Risk-Aversion Mechanism," *Judgment and Decision Making* 7, no. 1, 19. Simonsohn, Uri (2009), "Direct Risk Aversion: Evidence from Risky Prospects Valued Below Their Worst Outcome," *Psychological Science* 20, no. 6, 686–92. Wang, Y., T. Feng, and L. R. Keller (2013), "A Further Exploration of the Uncertainty Effect," *Journal of Risk and Uncertainty* 47, no. 3, 291–310. Yang, Y., J. Vosgerau, and G. Loewenstein (2013), "Framing Influences Willingness to Pay but Not Willingness to Accept," *Journal of Marketing Research* 50, no. 6, 725–38. Mislavsky, Robert, and Uri Simonsohn (2017), "When Risk Is Weird: Unexplained Transaction Features Lower Valuations," *Management Science* 64, no.11.

5. Tversky, Amos, and Eldar Shafir (1992), "The Disjunction Effect in Choice Under Uncertainty," *Psychological Science* 3, no. 5, 305–10.

6. It's important to remember that uncertainty isn't just about probabilities. A new product may have a fifty-fifty shot at being better than the old one, but beyond the actual chance that it will be better, people can still *feel* more or less certain. Take an election: supporters tend to feel certain that their candidate will win, even when the actual probabilities say otherwise. On the flip side, even if a new product or service has a high probability of being better, the uncertainty tax still makes people feel unsure about moving forward. So it's not enough just to change the actual probabilities. Sure, making a product or service that is better than the old one helps, but to change people's minds you have to make them feel more confident or certain, regardless of the actual probabilities.

7. Ducharme, L. J., H. K. Knudsen, P. M. Roman, and J. A. Johnson (2007), "Innovation Adoption in Substance Abuse Treatment: Exposure, Trialability, and the Clinical Trials Network," *Journal of Substance Abuse Treatment* 32, no. 4, 321–29. Mohamad Hsbollah, H., Kamil, and M. Idris (2009), "E-Learning Adoption: The Role of Relative Advantages, Trialability and Academic Specialisation," *Campus-Wide Information Systems* 26, no. 1, 54–70.

8. While trialability focuses on lowering the barriers to trial, reducing the barriers to continued action can also be valuable. Think about buying paper towels at the grocery store. Every time you run out of paper towels becomes a separate decision point. Do I want to buy the same brand (if I can even remember which one it was) or a different one? Contrast that with Netflix, gyms, or phone plans that rely on a subscription model. Rather than having to decide every month if you want to continue to use these services, they are set up so that you continue to be billed unless you tell them to stop. Thus, rather than the default being opt out, or the consumer having to do work at each point to buy the same brand, the default for these subscription models is opt in, or continue using until the customer says otherwise. Not surprisingly, opt-in models reduce the barrier to continued action and encourage people to keep doing the same thing over time.

9. Note that freemium only works if the offering is actually good. If it's buggy or underwhelming, people will try it, but they'll just switch back to what they were doing before.

10. Some companies also do a conditional version of free shipping. Spend more than $50, for example, and shipping is free. Not surprisingly, this isn't as motivating as unconditional free shipping, but it does encourage action. Almost half of consumers, for

example, report adding items to their cart to qualify for the offer. United Parcel Service of America, Inc. (2017), *UPS Pulse of the Online Shopper: A Customer Experience Study*. In many cases the cost of those items may be more than free shipping would have been in the first place.

11. Alina Tugend (2008), "'Two for One' . . . 'Free Delivery' . . . Hooked Yet?" *New York Times* (July 5).

12. Lowering the up-front cost can be applied to almost any situation. Pay-per-view channels often offer a free thirty-day trial. While this is a good place to start, giving away the first fifteen minutes of any program would be more effective. Once people have started watching a movie or a soccer game, their willingness to pay to watch the rest increases substantially. Want to get hotel guests to try the in-house restaurant? Give them a $25 credit for each day of their stay. Not only does it lower the cost of a trial meal, but it feels like a loss if they don't use it, so they're more likely to stop by.

13. Reducing the up-front cost also helps address the cost-benefit timing gap we talked about in the Endowment chapter. Not only are the costs of change usually now or soon, and the benefits later, but the benefits are more uncertain. Costs are pretty certain. New software costs a certain amount of money and at least some time to learn how to use. But the benefits are pretty uncertain. Will the new thing be better than the old? It's not clear, so why switch? But lowering the up-front cost helps close that gap. By moving experience up and often delaying the costs, the trial increases the chance that people will take action now.

14. Trying before buying is particularly useful for so-called experience goods, or cases where people need to experience something before they know if it is good for them. For search goods like printer cartridges or books, it's easier for customers to get a sense of fit by searching product specs or reading a description or reviews. But for things like shoes and mattresses, experience—and thus a trial— is vital.

15. Enterprising entrepreneurs have even applied this concept to more unusual settings. Rather than hoping customers stop by their barbershop, they bought an RV and drove around to local office parks, making it easier for busy professionals to get a haircut. Mobile car washes in Silicon Valley do the same thing. People might not take the time to get their car washed, but if it's right there in the parking lot, why not? By lowering discovery (and time) costs, these businesses encouraged consumers to give them a try and

boosted sales. Tax prep companies, financial advisors, and a host of other services could do something similar.

16. Peterson, J. Andrew, and V. Kumar (2010), "Can Product Returns Make You Money?" *MIT Sloan Review* (Spring).

17. Charging for shipping does have benefits. In addition to saving shipping costs, it decreases the likelihood of returns. If the person has to pay $6 to get the item back to you, they're not going to be as likely to send something back. So it's a win in a couple of respects. But these small wins are greatly overshadowed by the larger losses. Because people are savvy. They know that if they don't like something, the extra shipping costs will make them reticent to send it back. So what's simpler? Not ordering it at all. Waiting until you're exactly sure of what you want so you don't have to worry about returns. Or even simpler: ordering from a competitor who offers free shipping.

18. It is worth noting that making things reversible can sometimes lead people to like them less. A good deal of research shows that feeling you can return or swap out something later may interrupt people's natural tendency to make themselves happy with what they have. If I can just give it back if I don't like it, there's not as much need to like it in the first place. Consequently, if uncertainty is about the quality or effectiveness of the product or service itself, making something reversible is often beneficial. It allows people to see that the shoes fit or Dropbox is useful. But if the uncertainty is about individual preferences (e.g., am I the type of person who likes a lime-green sweater?), then it may be more likely to backfire.

19. Janakiraman, Narayan, Holly A. Syrdal, and Ryan Freling (2016), "The Effect of Return Policy Leniency on Consumer Purchase and Return Decisions: A Meta-Analytic Review," *Journal of Retailing* 92, no. 2, 226–35.

5. Corroborating Evidence

1. Pechmann, Cornelia, and David W. Stewart (1988), "Advertising Repetition: A Critical Review of Wearin and Wearout," *Current Issues and Research in Advertising* 11, nos. 1–2, 285–329.

2. Phil's parents stuck with it. When Phil tried to skip out of treatment and come back home, they said no. When he called them a couple days later asking for help, his father took him back to detox and said, "You're on your own." The detox staff told him they would help get him to the treatment center, but it was the last time

he could return to the center. (He'd been there six times.) Phil was mad, he was angry, but eventually he got clean.

3. Johnson, Vernon (1986), *Intervention: How to Help Someone Who Doesn't Want Help* (Center City, MN: Hazelden Foundation), 41.

4. Interventions work best when, rather than forcing addicts, they convince the addict themselves that it's time to change. Just as good negotiators don't jump to influence, the best interventionists don't start by asking addicts to get help. They start by simply asking them to listen. Rather than telling them what to do, the goal is to help them see their lives as they really are—to allow reality to shine through. To encourage the addicts to come around and internalize the fact that they need to change. Allowing them to chart their own path to your destination. They may still push back, or not want to go to treatment, but by encouraging them to begin to accept that there is a problem, they're more likely to get to a positive solution in the end.

5. Davis, Gerald F., and Henrich R. Greve (1997), "Corporate Elite Networks and Governance Changes in the 1980s," *American Journal of Sociology* 103, no. 1, 1–37. And Venkatesh, Viswanath (2006), "Where to Go from Here? Thoughts on Future Directions for Research on Individual-Level Technology Adoption with a Focus on Decision Making," *Decision Sciences* 37, no. 4, 497–518.

6. This multiple-source effect even extends to things like who communicates the information. In one study, participants were asked to listen to five positive reviews about a particular book. Compared to people who heard the same computerized voice read all five reviews, people who heard five different computerized voices read those reviews thought the book would be better and said they would be more likely to purchase it. Lee, Kwan Min (2004), "The Multiple Source Effect and Synthesized Speech," *Human Communication Research* 30, no. 2 (April 1), 182–207.

7. Platow, Michael J., S. Alexander Haslam, Amanda Both, Ivanne Chew, Michelle Cuddon, Nahal Goharpey, Jacqui Maurer, Simone Rosini, Anna Tsekouras, and Diana M. Grace (2005), "'It's Not Funny if They're Laughing': Self-Categorization, Social Influence, and Responses to Canned Laughter," *Journal of Experimental Social Psychology* 41, no 5, 542–50.

8. Dissimilar others can be valuable in some cases. When picking a nursing home for one's aging parent, for example, the perspective of a current resident is particularly valuable even if they're not like you.

9. Traag, Vincent A. (2016), "Complex Contagion of Campaign Donations," *PloS One* 11, no. 4, e0153539.

10. Aral, Sinan, and Christos Nicolaides (2017), "Exercise Contagion in a Global Social Network," *Nature Communications* 8 (article no. 14753).

11. Berger, Jonah, and Raghu Iyengar (2018), "How the Quantity and Timing of Social Influence Impact Behavior Change," Wharton Working Paper.

12. That said, there are certainly some situations where too much concentration can be negative. If people feel the concentration is manipulative or need time to think over a complex proposition, more time between exposures may be useful.

13. https://www.theatlantic.com/health/archive/2014/09/the-world-war-ii-campaign-to-bring-organ-meats-to-the-dinner-table/380737/.

14. Wansink, Brian (2002), "Changing Eating Habits on the Home Front: Lost Lessons from World War II Research," *Journal of Public Policy & Marketing* 21, no. 1, 90–99. Lewin, Kurt (1943), "Forces Behind Food Habits and Methods of Change," *Bulletin of the National Research Council* 108, no. 1043, 35–65. Romm, Cari (2014), "The World War II Campaign to Bring Organ Meats to the Dinner Table," *Atlantic* (September 25).

15. Lewin, Kurt (1951), *Field Theory in Social Science: Selected Theoretical Papers*, Dorwin Cartwright, ed. (New York: Harper & Brothers).

16. Wansink, Brian (2002), "Changing Eating Habits on the Home Front: Lost Lessons from World War II Research," *Journal of Public Policy and Marketing* 21(1), 90–99.

17. Lewin, Kurt (1947), "Group Decision and Social Change," *Readings in Social Psychology* 3, no. 1, 197–211.

Epilogue

1. Schroeder, J., and J. L. Risen (2016), "Befriending the Enemy: Outgroup Friendship Longitudinally Predicts Intergroup Attitudes in a Co-existence Program for Israelis and Palestinians," *Group Processes and Intergroup Relations* 19, 72–93.

2. Ross, Karen, and Ned Lazarus (2015), "Tracing the Long-Term Impacts of a Generation of Israeli–Palestinian Youth Encounters," *International Journal of Conflict Engagement and Resolution* 3, no. 2.

Appendix: Active Listening

1. Gardiner, James C. (1971), "A Synthesis of Experimental Studies of Speech Communication Feedback," *Journal of Communication* 21, no. 1 (March), 17–35.

2. Huang, Karen, Michael Yeomans, Alison Wood Brooks, Julia Minson, and Francesca Gino (2017), "It Doesn't Hurt to Ask: Question-Asking Increases Liking," *Journal of Personality and Social Psychology* 113, no. 3, 430–52.

Index

About the Author

Jonah Berger is a marketing professor at the Wharton School of the University of Pennsylvania and the internationally best-selling author of *Contagious* and *Invisible Influence*. He's a world-renowned expert on behavior change, social influence, word of mouth, and why products, ideas, and behaviors catch on. Berger has published more than fifty papers in top-tier academic journals, and popular accounts of his work often appear in publications such as the *New York Times, Wall Street Journal,* and *Harvard Business Review*. He often consults for companies like Google, Apple, Nike, and the Bill & Melissa Gates Foundation, and has helped hundreds of organizations drive new product adoption, shift public opinion, and change organizational culture. He's been named one of *Fast Company's* most creative people in business, and his work has been featured multiple times in the *New York Times Magazine's* "Year in Ideas."